18

CW01499529

CONVERGENCE
—IN PROPHECY—

for Judaism, Christianity,
Islam, and the Baha'i Faith

by

EILEEN MADDOCKS

JEWEL
PRESS
Burlington, Vermont

1844: Convergence in Prophecy
for Judaism, Christianity, Islam, and the Baha'i Faith
© 2018 by Eileen Maddocks

Library of Congress Control Number: 2018904819
ISBN 9781732106505 (Paperback)
ISBN 9781732106512 (eBook)

Publisher's Cataloging-In-Publication Data
(Prepared by The Donohue Group, Inc.)

Names: Maddocks, Eileen.
Title: 1844 : convergence in prophecy for Judaism, Christianity,
    Islam, and the Baha'i faith / by Eileen Maddocks.
Other Titles: Convergence in prophecy for Judaism, Christianity,
    Islam, and the Baha'i faith
Description: Burlington, Vermont : Jewel Press, [2018] | Includes
    bibliographical references and index.
Identifiers: ISBN 9781732106505 (paperback) |
    ISBN 9781732106512 (ebook)
Subjects: LCSH: Bahai Faith--History--19th century. | Prophecy-
    -History--19th century. | Religions--History--19th century.
    | Millerite movement--History--19th century. | Báb, 'Alī
    Muḥammad Shīrāzī, 1819-1850. | Bahá'u'lláh, 1817-1892.
Classification: LCC BP378 .S38 2018 (print) | LCC BP378 (ebook) |
    DDC 297.9315--dc23

Editing by JoAnn Gometz
Interior and Cover Design by Marina Kirsch

JEWEL
PRESS
Burlington, Vermont | jewelpress@outlook.com

Dedication

1962–2018

To the memory of my son,
Laird Anthony "Tony" Wilcox IV,
a wounded veteran who was a writer
like his mother and father.

CONTENTS

Acknowledgments

It takes a great deal of help to go the distance from entering the first words into the computer to finalizing a manuscript for publication. There are many people I want to thank.

Cyrus Parvini, the Producer and Executive Director of Radiant Century Productions, was an inspiration for me. He followed his vision to produce *The Miller Prediction*, a historical action feature film that explores the question of what happened in 1844.

I wrote a series of articles for *The Miller Prediction* website that provided historical background information for viewers of the film. Suellen Howley read them and commented that they could become a book. Indeed. She provided the spark for this book.

JoAnn Gometz, the copyeditor, found the gremlins, smoothed over the rocky patches, and made a lot of suggestions for improvements. Her work greatly enhanced this book.

It is said that a book should not be judged by its cover, but a cover is the reader's first impression of a book. Marina Kirsch, a graphic designer, produced this excellent cover, patiently working with me through all the decisions that had to be made. She also handled the interior design.

And last because an index is the final piece of work to be done, I thank Laura Shelley, a highly skilled indexer, for her diligence in creating the index for this book.

Writing can be lonely work. These friends and others shared my frustrations and joys during the process of creating this book. Team efforts can turn a chore into fun.

Foreword

With a grandfather who was a committed member of the Advent Christian Church and a mother who taught Bible history in a Universalist Church, I have always been interested in biblical prophecy and the Millerites—a mid-nineteenth century religious movement that foresaw the imminent return of Jesus Christ.

Imagine my joy when I discovered the book *Thief in the Night, or, The Strange Case of the Missing Millennium* by William Sears (1911–1992), a radio and television sports reporter in the 1940s and 1950s, who became intrigued by the phenomenon of Millerism—and its famous prediction that Jesus would return in 1844. Sears painstakingly scoured the Hebrew Bible and the New Testament for answers to the mystery of the return of Christ, which had been foretold but evidently had not happened. As a Catholic, Sears initially had no intention of looking for answers outside Christianity. However, as he dug for clues, his deeply inquiring mind found many references in the Jewish and Christian scriptures to events for which he was not looking and about which he knew nothing—the coming of the Báb and Bahá'u'lláh, the two Prophets of the Baha'i Faith. Leaving no prophetic stones unturned, Sears connected innumerable dots between Bible verses and Baha'i history and sacred texts, then presented the results of his thorough investigation and conclusions in his amazing book. Little could he have known at the outset that his detective skills would uncover a prophetic convergence in the year 1844 that brought together Judaism, Christianity, Islam, and the Baha'i Faith—and prompted Sears to become a Baha'i.

This book, *1844: Convergence in Prophecy for Judaism, Christianity, Islam, and the Baha'i Faith*, originated as a series of website articles I wrote to provide background information for viewers of the film *The Miller Prediction*. I expanded on these articles in order to more completely tell an exciting story that did not end in 1844. Actually, the year 1844 was just the beginning of a thrilling saga.

Although the year 1844 came and went with no indication of the return of Jesus, at least as far as the Millerite Christians could tell, several Protestant sects emerged to continue the expectation of the Second Coming. I've provided a brief overview of the emergence of the three denominations that arose directly from the Millerite movement and have survived to this day.

This book had to stay on track despite the opportunity to depart on intriguing tangents, so I could only summarize much of the available material about individual messianic movements that swept through Christianity and Islam. For a comprehensive work on the subject of the Millerite movement, I recommend the page-turner *Millennial Fever and the End of the World* by George R. Knight (b. 1941). He is a Seventh-day Adventist, historian, writer, and professor emeritus at Andrews University in Berrien, Michigan. Readers can also get further acquainted with William Miller, his correspondence, and the development of the movement through *Memoirs of William Miller* by Sylvester Bliss (1814–1863), who was a Millerite and close colleague of the man himself. LeRoy Froom (1890–1974), who was a Seventh-day Adventist minister and historian, wrote a comprehensive four-volume series *The Prophetic Faith of Our Fathers*. The third volume, *The Historical Development of Prophetic Interpretation*, covers the Adventist awakening in Europe and North America in the nineteenth century. In her book *The Half of It Was Never Told*, Carolyn Sparey Fox told the stories of three contemporaneous major figures in the messianic movements of the nineteenth century—William Miller in North America, Joseph Wolff in Europe and the Middle East, and Mulla Husayn in Persia.

One topic I could not cover in this book is the fascinating life of Joseph Wolff (1795–1862). Born a Jew in Bavaria, Germany, he left home at an early age, converted to Roman Catholicism, and then later became an Episcopalian. He was convinced that Jesus would return in 1847, but how he determined that date is not known. Wolff made two arduous missionary journeys throughout the Middle East and western Asia to convert Jews and Muslims to Christianity and to tell them about the coming Advent. Although he traveled in Persia and became acquainted with the Bábí movement, he neither recognized its significance nor gave it credence. And to put it mildly, Wolff had an irascible, intractable personality that seems to have precluded any lasting results from his missionary work.

An incredible phenomenon that I could not address here is that of the child preachers in Sweden in the early 1840s. In the evangelical Lutheran state church of the time, preaching contrary to the beliefs of the church was prohibited—not only did the church not emphasize the Second Coming of Jesus, but no one except the pastors was allowed to preach. However, many children and youth, some of whom could not read, began spontaneously preaching about the imminent coming of Christ. Thousands of Swedes listened to them and were moved by their message, which the young ones said came from the Holy Spirit. Even after receiving draconian punishments, these youth and children continued to deliver their message and received much press attention.

I've written *1844: Convergence in Prophecy* from my perspective as a Baha'i, a vantage point that may be new to many readers. Please set aside for the moment any previous understandings of traditional teachings—and even of Millerism—that you may have learned in synagogue, church, or mosque as you consider this different viewpoint. I encourage you to continue your own investigations of the ideas presented in *1844* through the websites and source materials provided in the notes and bibliography.

Unless otherwise indicated, I have used the New International Version (NIV) of the Bible for biblical quotations. The term Hebrew Bible is used instead of Old Testament out of respect for our spiritual forebears, whose heritage is not only relevant but surprisingly meaningful for us today. The user-friendly website Bible Gateway (www.BibleGateway.com) presents the Bible in more than 70 languages, including 50 English translations.

Quotations from the Bible and the Qur'an are italicized. In addition, quotations from the works of the Báb, Bahá'u'lláh, and 'Abdu'l-Bahá, the three Central Figures of the Baha'i Faith, and those of Shoghi Effendi are italicized.

When Arabic or Persian is translated into English, diacritical marks are used. These can be distracting for western readers. For ease of reading, diacritical marks are used only for the Báb, Bahá'u'lláh, 'Abdu'l-Bahá, the Qur'an, Bábí, and Baha'i, except when these marks are used in quotations.

In addition to BCE (Before the Common Era) and CE (the Common Era) to designate Jewish and Christian dates, a few dates from Islamic history are given as AH (Anno Hegirae, meaning "in the year of Muhammad's Hegira"). This era began in the year 622 CE when Muhammad and His followers fled from Mecca to Medina to escape persecution, a flight called the Hegira.

Prophets with a capital "P" are the Prophets of God, also called the Manifestations or Messengers of God, while prophets with a small "p" are the classical prophets of the Hebrew Bible.

The Baha'i Faith is sometimes referred to as "the Faith."

Some of the books and articles cited in the endnotes are available online and relevant URLs are provided in the bibliography.

Introduction

The religious movement called Adventism swept North America and Europe in the early decades of the nineteenth century, bringing fervor and urgency to the expectation of the imminent return of Jesus Christ. At the time, the movement came to be known in the United States and Europe as Millerism, named after William Miller, a Baptist farmer in upstate New York who assiduously studied biblical timelines and prophecies for clues about when Jesus would return—an event called the Second Coming. Miller, though, was just one of many Christian clergy and lay people who had been independently studying the Bible for details about that very topic since the turn of the century. The Second Coming had always been a part of Christian theology, but interest in it ebbed and flowed through the centuries. Adventism caught fire as students of the Bible calculated that the prophet Daniel had pointed to the years 1843 or 1844 for this blessed event. They collaborated to investigate the prophecies and generally agreed with one another's findings. So, when nothing happened in 1843, the scholars decided that they had made an error by assuming the presence of a "zero year" between BCE and CE. New calculations eliminated this extra year and identified the early days in 1844 up to March 21 as the time of the Advent. Again, nothing happened. The scholars went back to the biblical prophecies once more and concluded that the date of the Second Coming would be October 22, 1844. However, that day also came and went with no signs of the event. The ensuing widespread emotional and religious distress was deemed the Great Disappointment.

Nevertheless, the biblical prophecies about the return of Christ upon which Millerism was largely based, especially those in the book of Daniel, Chapter 8, Verses 1–14, turned out to be surprisingly accurate. Millerite scholars had calculated the right year—on the wrong continent!

In any case, Miller and his fellow biblical scholars could not have understood the meanings of Daniel's prophecies because the prophet himself had been told that they could not be interpreted before their appointed time: *"Go your way, Daniel, because the words are rolled up and sealed until the time of the end."* (Daniel 12:9) The time did, indeed, turn out to be 1844, but only in retrospect are the meanings of Daniel's predictions apparent.

Christian expectations for the imminent return of Jesus in the Western world formed just one part of the picture. Unknown in the West, a similar quest was underway in the Shia Islamic Middle East. Therefore, a basic understanding of two religions that emerged in Persia in the mid-1800s is a necessary foundation for the concepts explored in this book.

While Christians in the West expected the return of Jesus, Shia Muslims in Persia and Iraq expected the imminent return of the twelfth Imam, who was called the Qa'im (the Risen One), or Mahdi [Imám-Mihdí]. According to Shia tradition, the twelfth Imam was the last of the legitimate spiritual successors to Muhammad who possessed divine knowledge and authority and were responsible for interpreting the Qur'an and giving spiritual guidance. The twelfth Imam was believed to have disappeared in the year 874 CE under mysterious and disputed circumstances. Shia tradition maintains that he remained alive throughout the centuries in a state of occultation, hidden from the world, and that he would return when the time was right to establish the kingdom of God on earth.

In Persia, a group of Shia Muslims led by two Islamic scholars and teachers believed that a new and independent Revelation, as attested and foreshadowed by the sacred scriptures of Islam, would soon be given. These religious scholars were searching for the Prophet who would bring that Revelation. In some ways, the two expectations in the East and the West were parallel.

Perhaps the foremost Islamic searcher was Mulla[1] Husayn (1813–1849), who arrived in Shiraz, Persia, to a warm welcome from a stranger on the evening of May 22, 1844. After conversation and hospitality, his host, a young merchant named Mírzá 'Ali Muhammad-i-Shírází (1819-1850) proclaimed to Mulla Husayn that He was the Prophet of his search. He called Himself the Báb, which in English means the Gate of God. The word "gate" is an English translation of the Arabic word *báb*. The Báb later wrote:

It is clear and evident that the object of all preceding Dispensations hath been to pave the way for the advent of Muhammad, the Apostle of God. These, including the Muhammadan Dispensation, have had, in their turn, as their objective the Revelation proclaimed by the Qá'im. The purpose underlying this Revelation, as well as those that preceded it, has, in like manner, been to announce the advent of the Faith of Him Whom God will make manifest. And this Faith—the Faith of Him Whom God will make manifest—in its turn, together with all the Revelations gone before it, have as their object the Manifestation destined to succeed it. And the latter, no less than all the Revelations preceding it, prepare the way for the Revelation which is yet to follow. The process of the rise and setting of the Sun of Truth will thus indefinitely continue—a process that hath had no beginning and will have no end.[2]

The mission of the Báb was twofold—to make a complete break with Islam, thus setting the stage for a new spiritual era, and to proclaim the coming of *"Him Whom God will make manifest."* In that way, He both brought an entirely new Revelation from God and served as the Herald for the Revelation of Bahá'u'lláh to follow. The Báb had complete love and respect for the Qur'an, as well as an intimate knowledge of that book. In no way did His declaration denigrate the Qur'an or the true essence of Islam. On the contrary, the Báb initiated a fulfillment of many references in the Qur'an to the coming of a new era and it validated the Qur'an's divine truths.

A new religion thus emerged from the milieu of Shia Islam, just as Christianity had arisen from that of Judaism. The Báb announced that humanity stood at the threshold of a new era of spiritual and moral reformation and on the cusp of a soon-to-be-revealed second Divine Revelation.

Fanatical Islamic clergy fiercely opposed the Báb, just as the Jewish priesthood had opposed Jesus and the idolatrous Meccans had opposed Muhammad. Under the direction of the clergy and their allies in power, the Báb was imprisoned for about half of his six-year ministry while His disciples and followers were being persecuted, with many imprisoned or murdered throughout Persia for accepting the Bábí Faith or teaching it. The Báb was executed by a firing squad in Tabriz, Persia, in 1850. The ministry of the Báb lasted six years from 1844 to 1850. His Dispensation lasted nine years, from May 1844 to late in 1852, the shortest span in history for a divinely revealed religion. Throughout that time, the Báb repeatedly foretold that *"Him Whom God will make manifest"* would appear at the end of those nine years. He urged his followers to watch and recognize that individual when He appeared and to follow His guidance and teachings.

Among the early followers of the Báb was a young nobleman of high social standing, Mírzá Husayn-'Alí Núrí (1817–1892). He taught the new Bábí Faith, earning wide recognition for His wisdom and respect for His role as one of the Bábí movement's most influential believers. He was tortured and imprisoned in 1852 for four months in the infamous underground prison, the Siyah-Chal. While chained there in perpetual darkness, He was visited by the Holy Spirit and was told that He was the one whom the Báb had prophesied, *"Him Whom God will make manifest,"* the next Messenger of God. However, Mírzá Husayn-'Alí, known as Bahá'u'lláh, which is Arabic for the Glory of God, did not openly divulge this information at that time. After four months of incarceration in the appalling pit, the Persian government persuaded Ottoman authorities to accept Him in exile in Ottoman-controlled Baghdad. As the son of a *vizier*, or minister, in the court of the Shah, He could not be executed.

The year 1852 was the first of forty years of exile and imprisonment for Bahá'u'lláh. To the consternation of the Shah, Persian authorities, and their Ottoman allies, Bahá'u'lláh continued to attract attention in Baghdad as a spiritual leader. The Persian government persuaded the Ottoman authorities to exile Him in 1863 further away to Constantinople (now Istanbul), Turkey, and a few months later to Adrianople (now Edirne). Bahá'u'lláh lived in Baghdad for ten years. Just days before His departure from the city He openly announced that He was the Messenger of God foretold by the Báb. Th   e year was 1863, nineteen years after the Báb's own proclamation in 1844.

During His time in Adrianople, Bahá'u'lláh wrote a series of letters, called tablets, to the world's major religious and political leaders.[3] In them, He proclaimed His station and wrote about the dawn of a new age of universal peace. He also warned the recipients that cataclysmic upheavals in the world's political, religious, and social order would precede the new age if they ignored His teachings and admonitions. In other words, based on their actions and decisions, the rulers could achieve peace relatively easily, or humanity would have to attain it the hard way. We know which path was chosen.

Bahá'u'lláh's detractors in Persia continued to agitate against Him and His followers, despite their exile. In 1868, the Ottoman authorities responded by sending Bahá'u'lláh from Adrianople to His final destination, the dreaded penal colony and prison fortress in the walled city of Akka (Akko, Acre) in Ottoman-ruled Palestine. The conditions of His initial harsh imprisonment were gradually eased as various Turkish authorities and Islamic clergy in Akka became His devoted admirers. In 1877, He was even allowed to live outside the city in a country home and to freely receive guests. One of those visitors was Edward Granville Browne, an orientalist at Cambridge University, who met Bahá'u'lláh in 1890. That encounter inspired Browne to write a "pen portrait" of Bahá'u'lláh. (See Appendix A)

A prolific writer, Bahá'u'lláh sometimes recorded divine revelation with His own pen, but more often He delivered it through dictation that kept three or four secretaries busy at a time. The scope of His writings in both Arabic and Persian encompasses an uncountable number of subjects found in more than 18,000 unique, authenticated works comprising about six million words. In fact, His writings are referred to as the "Ocean of His Word." About 15,000 of these writings, together with the works of the Báb, 'Adu'l-Bahá, and Shoghi Effendi, are held in the International Baha'i Archives at the Baha'i World Centre in state-of-the-art environmental conditions.[4] They form the centerpiece in an ongoing process of collection, collation, and authentication. To this day, the descendants of individuals who received tablets from the Báb and Bahá'u'lláh are still turning these precious documents over to the Baha'i World Centre, thus necessitating continuous revisions of the numbers. Portions of these works have been translated into more than eight hundred languages.

A press release from the *Baha'i World News Service* emphasized the extent of the writings of Bahá'u'lláh, as well as their nearness to our time, when it announced the publication of *The Summons of the Lord of Hosts*, a compilation of Bahá'u'lláh's tablets to the leading rulers of His time:

> Titled *The Summons of the Lord of Hosts*, the 272-page book contains authoritative English translations of six major works written by Bahá'u'lláh in the latter half of the 19th century. Collectively, the works clearly enunciate Bahá'u'lláh's claim to prophethood and offer a prescription for peaceful and just leadership in the modern world.
>
> The collected volume represents only a fraction of Bahá'u'lláh's output during His 40-year ministry, when He revealed thousands of tablets which altogether represent a volume more than 70 times the size of the Qur'an and more than 15 times the size of the Old and New Testaments of the Bible.
>
> Not only is the size of the revelation significant, but also—thanks in part to access to both original documents and the historical context in which they were revealed—the Baha'i Faith has a much more direct link to its origins than is enjoyed by most other religions.[5]

In addition, archivists have preserved countless eyewitness accounts of the events surrounding the lives and activities of the Báb, Bahá'u'lláh, and their contemporaries. Humanity is extraordinarily fortunate that these two Prophets came so relatively recently in history. Scholars of the Baha'i Faith will probably never have to study ancient languages, trace scripture through successive translations, or resort to deduction and conjecture, as biblical scholars have been forced to do. The Baha'i Faith and its sacred texts are part of modern history.

Bahá'u'lláh passed away in 1892. In his will, He appointed as His successor His eldest son, 'Abbás Effendi (1844–1921). With that role came the responsibility to serve as the head of the nascent Baha'i Faith and also as the only authorized interpreter of the writings of both Bahá'u'lláh and the Báb.

Early in life, 'Abbás Effendi took for himself the name 'Abdu'l-Bahá, an Arabic title that translates as *servant* ('Abdu'l) of the *glory* (Bahá). It was a way of recognizing his dedication to his father, which began even before 'Abdu'l-Bahá accompanied his father and family into exile at age nine and shared His father's decades of imprisonment. He expressed the meaning of his name as follows:

> *My name is 'Abdu'l-Bahá, my identity is 'Abdu'l-Bahá, my qualification is 'Abdu'l-Bahá, my reality is 'Abdu'l-Bahá, my praise is 'Abdu'l-Bahá. Thraldom to the Blessed Perfection is my glorious and refulgent diadem; and servitude to all the human race is my perpetual religion. No name, no title, no mention, no commendation hath he nor will ever have except 'Abdu'l-Bahá. This is my longing. This is my supreme apex. This is my greatest yearning. This is my eternal life. This is my everlasting glory!*[6]

'Abdu'l-Bahá's imprisonment under the Ottoman terms of custody continued sixteen years beyond his father's death. After living a total of fifty-six years as a prisoner in exile, he was finally freed in 1908, along with all of the Ottoman Empire's religious and political prisoners, when the Young Turks Revolution restored the 1876 constitution and ushered in multi-party politics and social reforms. 'Abdu'l-Bahá had guided the development of the Faith throughout the years after the passing of Bahá'u'lláh. Under his leadership, the Faith expanded from the Middle East into Asia, Africa, Europe, and North America. At the same time, 'Abdu'l-Bahá devoted much of his ministry to serving the poor in Akka and its neighboring city across the bay, Haifa.

'Abdu'l-Bahá was also a prolific writer both before and after his release, penning three books and carrying on a vast and diverse correspondence. More than 30,000 unique works, comprising over five million words, are saved in the International Baha'i Archives.[7] In addition, several compilations of 'Abdu'l-Bahá's talks and writings have been published as books.[8]

After his release, 'Abdu'l-Bahá undertook a grueling three-year (1911–1913) tour through Europe, Canada, and the United States. He foresaw the coming of World War I. Upon his return to Palestine, he worked tirelessly to promote the cultivation and storage of grain crops to feed the populace during the coming conflict. He stayed in Palestine throughout the war, continuing both his local work for the poor and his guidance of the international Baha'i community despite Allied bombardments and threats from the Turkish commander to crucify him on Mount Carmel, the steep slope on which much of Haifa stands. In gratitude for his humanitarian efforts during the war, the British Mandate of Palestine awarded 'Abdu'l-Bahá a knighthood (KBE) in April 1920.

'Abdu'l-Bahá died eighteen months later in November 1921. Thousands of mourners followed his casket from his home in Haifa to the Shrine of the Báb on Mount Carmel, where he was laid to rest in a burial chamber next to that of the Báb. Six speakers from the Christian, Muslim, and Jewish communities gave eulogies. The remains of the Báb had been transported from Persia to Haifa very quietly many years after His execution. Bahá'u'lláh had designated to 'Abdu'l-Bahá precisely where the Báb was to be interred on Mount Carmel. 'Abdu'l-Bahá planned and started the construction of the Shrine of the Báb, which was finished by his grandson, Shoghi Effendi.

The Will and Testament of 'Abdu'l-Bahá named twin successors—the Universal House of Justice, which had not yet been elected, and a Guardian of the Faith, his eldest grandson, Shoghi Effendi Abbás (1897–1957). He also designated Shoghi Effendi the sole interpreter of the writings of the Báb and Bahá'u'lláh.

Shoghi Effendi was educated at the American School in Beirut, Lebanon, and at Oxford University, England. He had a brilliant mind and was self-disciplined beyond measure. He was also another prolific writer in Arabic and Persian—and in English, a language of which he had an exquisite, erudite, and compelling command. His written words offered profound insights into the spiritual dimensions of civilization and the dynamics of social change.[9] More than 22,000 of his unique works have been identified and most have been authenticated.[10] With infinite patience, Shoghi Effendi gradually unveiled an awe-inspiring vision of the spiritual future toward which humanity is evolving. At the same time, he guided the progress of the Faith with painstaking attention, one small victory at a time, as it spread globally. He labored without pause for the development of the buildings and gardens of the Baha'i World Centre on the slopes of Mount Carmel in Haifa, a city that became part of the newly formed nation of Israel during his lifetime. He also translated many of the works of the Báb and Bahá'u'lláh into English.

Then, in November 1957, Shoghi Effendi's passing left the Baha'i world bereft. The love that the Baha'i world had for him was reflected in his often being referred to as the "beloved Guardian." In addition, it had been impossible for Shoghi Effendi to appoint his successor in accordance with the provisions of the Will and Testament of 'Adu'l-Bahá. This situation presented an obscure question that was not covered in the Sacred Writings and could only be referred to the Universal House of Justice. But this institution would not be elected for another six years.

Fortunately, Shoghi Effendi had continued the practice instituted by Bahá'u'lláh, and followed by 'Abdu'l-Bahá, of recognizing specific individuals for their tireless devotion to the protection and expansion of the Baha'i Faith and designating them Hands of the Cause of God. In a letter sent to the Baha'is of the World a month before his death, Shoghi Effendi announced:

> … yet another step in the progressive unfoldment of one of the cardinal and pivotal institutions ordained by Bahá'u'lláh, and confirmed in the Will and Testament of 'Abdu'l-Bahá, involving the designation of yet another contingent of the Hands of the Cause of God, raising thereby to thrice nine the total number of the Chief Stewards of Bahá'u'lláh's embryonic World Commonwealth, who have been invested by the unerring Pen of the Center of His Covenant with the dual function of guarding over the security, and of insuring the propagation, of His Father's Faith.[11]

All but one of the surviving twenty-seven members of the institution of the Hands of the Cause met in the mansion of Bahji in Akka soon after the funeral for

Shoghi Effendi. They elected nine of their number to conduct the affairs of the Faith from the Baha'i World Centre in Haifa. This decision was subsequently endorsed unanimously by the National Spiritual Assemblies. The nine Hands operated under the legal title "The Custodians of the Baha'i World Faith."[12]

The Universal House of Justice wrote in 1965 that the safest course of action for the Hands had been

> ... to follow with undeviating firmness the instructions and policies of Shoghi Effendi. The entire history of religion shows no comparable record of such strict self-discipline, such absolute loyalty and such complete self-abnegation by the leaders of a religion finding themselves suddenly deprived of their divinely inspired guide. The debt of gratitude which mankind for generations, nay, ages to come, owes to this handful of grief-stricken, steadfast, heroic souls is beyond estimation. The Guardian had given the Bahá'í world explicit and detailed plans covering the period until Ridván 1963 [April 21–May 2, 1963], the end of the Ten Year Crusade. From that point onward, unless the Faith were to be endangered, further divine guidance was essential. This was the second pressing reason for the calling of the election of the Universal House of Justice. The rightness of the time was further confirmed by references in Shoghi Effendi's letters to the Ten Year Crusade's being followed by other plans under the direction of the Universal House of Justice.[13]

The Hands of the Cause had been an obvious choice for administering the affairs of the Faith from 1957 to 1963 and overseeing the completion of the Ten Year Plan, and then calling for the first election of the Universal House of Justice. They had been designated by Shoghi Effendi as the *"Chief Stewards of Bahá'u'lláh's embryonic World Commonwealth."*[14]

In 1963, members of the fifty-six National Spiritual Assemblies in existence cast secret ballots to elect the first Universal House of Justice, the international governing body of the Faith. All of the Hands had declared themselves ineligible for election. The highest institution of the Faith, the Universal House of Justice, is comprised of nine members who are elected every five years by members of all National Spiritual Assemblies. The nine-member National Spiritual Assemblies themselves are elected by the Baha'is of their countries. The Universal House of Justice is responsible for applying the principles of the Faith within the global Baha'i community, protecting the Faith from those who wish it harm, teaching the Faith in various global endeavors, and administering the affairs of the worldwide community.

Baha'is accept the divine authority of the successorship of 'Abdu'l-Bahá, Shoghi Effendi, and then the Universal House of Justice. This is the first time in the history of revealed religions that a Covenant of succession—a provision for the protection and leadership of a new faith—has been enacted and has prevented schism into competing sects. The many decades of adherence to the Covenant provided the stability for the six-year transition from 1957 to 1963 that was marked by the continued expansion of the Faith. The 1963 election of the first Universal House of Justice represents the continuation of the Baha'i Covenant. The Faith is undivided and free of schism. Therefore, it can work effectively and credibly for global unity.

As discussed above, most of the original, handwritten writings of the Báb and Bahá'u'lláh are extant and carefully secured at the International Baha'i Archives. This is the first time in human history that the original handwritten words of Prophets of God have been preserved. In addition, most of 'Abdu'l-Baha's writings and all of Shoghi Effendi's writings have been saved. Much of this trove of religious literature has been published in several languages and is readily available to anyone who wants to study it.

Bahá'u'lláh came for many reasons. The foremost was to unify humanity. The foundational teaching of the Baha'i Faith is the oneness of God, the oneness of the Prophets of God, and the oneness of humanity. All of creation is one, as scientists now understand from their studies of physics, biology, and the havoc wreaked upon the earth by climate change.

Next to unity is the importance of justice, upon which future societies must be based. On that topic Bahá'u'lláh wrote:

> O SON OF SPIRIT! The best beloved of all things in My sight is Justice; turn not away therefrom if thou desirest Me, and neglect it not that I may confide in thee. By its aid thou shalt see with thine own eyes and not through the eyes of others, and shalt know of thine own knowledge and not through the knowledge of thy neighbor. Ponder this in thy heart; how it behooveth thee to be. Verily justice is My gift to thee and the sign of My loving-kindness. Set it then before thine eyes.[15]

Bahá'u'lláh also explained that God has sent and will continue to send a series of Prophets to educate mankind.

Each Prophet repeats the spiritual verities of the previous Prophets, but also brings new teachings, abrogates outmoded social and religious laws, and reveals new ones suited to the times. Humanity has evolved from the spiritual and emotional level of children and is now in its tumultuous adolescence, poised to move into adulthood.

These Prophets appear in cycles. The Adamic Cycle, also called the Prophetic Cycle, lasted for approximately six thousand years from the Prophet Adam through the Dispensation of the Prophet Muhammad. The Báb and Bahá'u'lláh initiated the Cycle of Fulfillment during which mankind is destined to come of age spiritually.

CHAPTER 1

Moving to Fever Pitch

The evangelical and religious revitalization of the First Great Awakening swept Europe and the American colonies, especially in the Northeast. Peaking in the 1730s and '40s, the First Great Awakening gave rise to John Wesley and evangelical Methodism, a reaction to the Episcopal Church. Methodism achieved its name through its emphasis on logic and reason, a spiritual method of living. Methodism negated the need for ceremony and church hierarchy, stressing instead that faith was an intensely personal matter that fostered spiritual conviction and redemption, or salvation, only through Jesus Christ. Not only was self-study of the Bible paramount, but Methodism called for preaching the gospel outside the confines of any established church. This was a step far beyond Martin Luther.

This new freedom for every person not only to study but to preach, and the evangelical nature of early Methodism, gave rise to the itinerant minister. "Circuit riders ... held a hallowed place in Methodist history and mythology. Missionary work was the hallmark of early Methodism and its first institutionalized form were the circuit riders or itinerant preachers. They were the new St. Pauls in the Methodist pantheon. ... In some ways, after 1740, these itinerants may be viewed as an invading army violating the home or parish of the established Anglican Church."[1] Whether ordained ministers or lay preachers with limited education, these circuit riders paved the way for the waves of itinerant Millerite and other preachers of the Second Great Awakening of the nineteenth century.

While Wesley and the Methodists reinforced the belief in the return of Jesus, called the Second Coming, few tried to project a date for the event. Those who did attracted few followers. Many Christians expected the Second Coming to be a literal return of Jesus in the same body He had inhabited so many centuries before. They also expected His return to be marked by the occasion of the Last Judgment when the living and the dead would be sorted toward heaven or hell.

Adventism was inherently part of Christian theology because Jesus said He would return. The book of Matthew, Chapter 24, verses 1–51, contains a long discourse from Jesus to His disciples about His return. Here He told them that disasters and turmoil, wars and the rumors of wars, would precede His return. However, He disclaimed any knowledge of the timing: *"But about that day or hour no one knows, not even the angels in heaven, nor the Son, but only the Father."* (Matthew 24:36)

Jesus did, however, give one hint: *"So when you see standing in the holy place 'the abomination that causes desolation,' spoken of through the prophet Daniel—let the reader understand ..."* (Matthew 24:15) What was "the abomination that causes desolation"? It would be a long wait to find out because the words of Daniel were *"rolled up and sealed until the time of the end."* (Daniel 12:9)

Not even a hundred years after the First Great Awakening commenced, the Second Great Awakening began. Many students of the Bible undertook serious investigation of the return, mostly working alone. They calculated possible dates for the Advent from biblical prophecies. An atmosphere of religious expectancy spread as these students found each other and began to collaborate. By the 1830s, Adventism, the expectation of the Second Coming, roared through English and American Protestantism. Adventist believers expected the *imminent* return of Jesus Christ.

What lit the fire for the Second Great Awakening? Natural phenomena that seemed highly irregular, or even supernatural, for one. In the American Northeast, people experienced the "Dark Day" of 1780 when raging wildfires in Canada produced smoke that totally obscured the sun.

Then came the "year without a summer," 1816. Europe and North America had a normal spring, but hard frosts hit throughout the normally hot season. Crop failures caused widespread hunger. Unknown to either Europeans or Americans at the time, the Pacific volcano of Mount Tambora had erupted in massive fashion that April, spewing so much ash that it obscured the sun half a globe away. During that awful summer, a group of writers including Lord Byron, Percy Shelley, and Shelley's future wife, Mary Wollstonecraft Godwin, challenged each other to write horrid tales inspired by the dark and frosty season—one was Mary Shelley's classic, *Frankenstein*.

On November 12, 1833, a spectacular meteor shower of previously unseen scale, the Leonids from the Comet Tempel-Tuttle, filled the sky over the eastern United

States. An estimated 240,000 "falling stars" rained down for several hours. This spectacular, frightening display seemed to fulfill the words of Isaiah as told by Jesus:

> Immediately after the distress of those days
> 'the sun will be darkened, and the moon will not
>   give its light;
> the stars will fall from the sky, and the heavenly
>   bodies will be shaken.'
> (Matthew 24:29, quoting Isaiah 13:20 and 34:4)

The Second Great Awakening reached fever pitch in the United States in the early 1840s. It was a turning away from Deism, which was the belief that God was impersonal and that man should rely on rational thinking. It was also a repudiation of church liturgy and structure and an embrace of evangelical Christianity. Church membership increased dramatically. All Protestant denominations of the time, except perhaps the Quaker and Universalist, believed in the physical return of Christ to earth for the final judgment of the living and the dead and the establishment of a reign of righteousness. But now there was a growing emphasis on when Jesus would return although He had said that only the Father knew:

> Therefore keep watch, because you do not know on what day your Lord will come. But understand this: If the owner of the house had known at what time of night the thief was coming, he would have kept watch and would not have let his house be broken into. So you also must be ready, because the Son of Man will come at an hour when you do not expect him. (Matthew 24:42–43)

Enter William Miller (1782–1849), a farmer and Baptist lay preacher in Low Hampton, New York, just across the border from Vermont. The oldest of sixteen children, he had a conventional childhood. He was raised in a devout Baptist farm household with a grandfather and several other relatives who were ministers and preachers. Miller's mother taught him to read, but his formal education was limited to three months each winter during his school years. He was an avid reader of the few books belonging to the family and those that he could borrow. His early, burning desire to learn and his wide reading of various subjects helped form his eloquent, thoughtful writing as an adult.

Surprisingly, considering his Baptist origins and his later pioneering effort in Adventism, Miller spent fourteen years of his early adulthood embracing Deism, an outgrowth of the Age of Enlightenment that rejected the Bible as the standard of religious truth. Miller questioned for many years the Christian doctrines taught to him in childhood and rejected the idea of divine revelation. Instead, he studied the writings of Voltaire, Thomas Paine, Ethan Allen, Benjamin Franklin, and other Deist thinkers who held the belief that God had created the world and then let His creation evolve on its own. Human observation and reasoning were sufficient for a rational life, they suggested. Deist attitudes about life after death ran the gamut from a belief in an afterlife as a natural part of human creation, with suitable rewards and punishments for conduct in this life, to a certainty that the grave was the end of one's existence. Even though Miller identified with the intellectuals who favored Deism, he faithfully accompanied his wife and children to the local

Baptist church services. His livelihood was farming. His social life revolved around the Masonic Order in which he attained the highest degree available in his area. His passions were reading and studying.

Miller was also a patriot. His father served as a captain in the Revolutionary War and the younger Miller joined the Vermont militia as a lieutenant in 1810. He had been promoted to the rank of captain in the United States Army by 1813. During the War of 1812, he fought at the pivotal battle of Plattsburgh, a small town in New York on the western shore of Lake Champlain, a short distance south of the Canadian border.

As the years passed, Miller found less and less comfort in Deism. He seemed to have long embraced the nihilistic belief that life ended at the grave. However, the wartime death of a close friend named Spencer brought forth nagging doubts about his beliefs and prompted him to write the following anguished words in a letter to his wife:

> But a short time, and, like Spencer, I shall be no more. It is a solemn thought. Yet, could I be sure of one other life, there would be nothing terrific; but to go out like an extinguished taper is insupportable—the thought is doleful. No! Rather let me cling to that hope which warrants a never-ending existence; a future spring, where troubles shall cease, and tears find no conveyance; where never-ending spring shall flourish, and love, pure as the driven snow, rest in every breast.[2]

Miller wrote of that time in his memoirs:

> Annihilism was a cold and chilling thought, and accountability was a sure destruction to all. The

heavens were as brass over my head, and the earth as iron under my feet. *Eternity!—what was it? And death—why was it?* The more I reasoned, the further I was from demonstration. The more I thought, the more scattered were my conclusions. I tried to stop thinking, but my thoughts would not be controlled. I was truly wretched, but did not understand *the cause.* I murmured and complained, but knew not of whom. I knew that there was a wrong, but knew not how or where to find the right. I mourned, but without hope.[3]

Epiphany came for Miller in 1816 while he was delivering a talk in church. It happened as a startling mystical experience, an intense inner vision that he described as follows:

Suddenly the character of a Saviour was vividly impressed upon my mind. It seemed that there might be a Being so good and compassionate as to himself atone for our transgressions, and thereby save us from suffering the penalty of sin. I immediately felt how lovely such a Being must be, and imagined that I could cast myself into the arms of, and trust in the mercy of, such an One. But the question arose, How can it be proved that such a Being does exist? Aside from the Bible, I found that I could get no evidence of the existence of such a Saviour, or even of a future state … I was constrained to admit that the Scriptures must be a revelation from God … The Bible now became my chief study, and I can truly say, I searched it with great delight. I found the half was never told me … I lost all taste for other reading, and applied my heart to get wisdom from God.[4]

Miller embarked on an intensive, disciplined study of the Bible, starting with Genesis and comparing verse with verse as he went along. For the rest of his life, Miller studied only the Bible, aided by *Cruden's Concordance*.[5] He became convinced that the Bible was its own interpreter and that its parables and metaphors were either understandable within their immediate connection or elsewhere in the Bible, in which cases the explanations showed them to be literally true— unless the explanations were symbolic, such as the term "day" given in certain prophetic utterances. The Bible was for Miller a system of revealed truths, simply and clearly given, to be understood with common sense, at least with what he construed to be common sense. As Methodism sought methodical order, Millerism would pursue a rational approach.

Miller was especially interested in biblical prophecies and came to believe that all of them had been or would be literally fulfilled. Along with many other biblical scholars of his day, Miller took the prophecies of Daniel to heart, especially Daniel 8:14: *"He [a holy one] said to me, 'It will take 2,300 evenings and mornings; then the sanctuary will be reconsecrated.'"*

By 1822, Miller believed that he understood the various prophecies about the return of Jesus Christ. He wrote: "With the solemn conviction that such momentous events were predicted in the Scriptures, to be fulfilled in so short a space of time, the question came home to me with mighty power regarding my duty to the world, in view of the evidence that had affected my own mind. If the end was so near, it was important that the world should know it."[6]

That year Miller wrote a partial summary of his articles of faith, which was later found among his papers and had not been published during his lifetime. Article XV states, "I believe that the Second Coming of Jesus Christ is near, even at the door, even within twenty-one years—on or before 1843."[7] He also wrote, "When I was about my business, it was continually ringing in my ears, 'Go and tell the world of their danger.'"[8] For nine years, he battled with this voice.

Miller's life as a farmer, biblical scholar, Sunday school teacher, and community leader was full. Only in 1831 did he begin to share his apocalyptic views about the imminent return of Jesus, and only with reluctance after much procrastination, hesitation, and inner struggling with God. For years, he had heard the message "Go and tell the world" and he could no longer ignore the summons:

> I did all I could to avoid the conviction that anything was required of me; and I thought that by freely speaking of it to all, I would freely perform my duty, and that God would raise up the necessary instrumentality for the accomplishment of the work. I prayed that some minister might see the truth, and devote himself to its promulgation; but still it was impressed on me, "Go and tell it to the world: their blood will I require at thy hand." I tried to excuse myself to the Lord for not going out and proclaiming it to the world. I told the Lord that I was not used to public speaking; that I had not the necessary qualifications to gain the attention of an audience; that I was very diffident, and feared to go

before the world; that they would "not believe me or hearken to my voice;" that I was "slow of speech and of a slow tongue." But I could get no relief.[9]

Finally, Miller gave an ultimatum to God: He would not go and speak unless he was invited! What a relief he felt! Surely no one would invite him to speak in public. But his relief was very short-lived. Within half an hour, Miller's nephew from Dresden, a town sixteen miles away, arrived and said that the minister would be away that Sunday. Would Miller speak in Dresden on the Second Coming? To feel more comfortable, he could even speak in his sister's home instead of the church. So that was that. In August 1831, the Baptists in Dresden turned out to hear Miller speak and the Millerite movement took off from there. Miller was granted a license to preach by the Baptist Church in 1833 although he was never ordained. By 1835, he had turned the farm over to his sons and started devoting himself to preaching his message of the Second Coming full-time.

By the accounts of the day, Miller was not a charismatic preacher. His sermons and lectures often lasted two hours and were not of a tone to create hysteria. On the contrary, he was homely in appearance and plodding in ungrammatical speech, although he was also very rational, thorough, and compelling in his presentations. Sylvester Bliss (1814–1863), one of Miller's colleagues and a Millerite minister and editor in his own right, described Miller as:

> ... a good citizen, a kind neighbor, an affectionate husband and parent, and a devoted Christian; good to the poor and benevolent as objects of charity were presented; in the Sunday-school

was teacher and superintendent; in the church he performed important service as a reader and exhorter, and, in support of religious worship, no other member, perhaps, did as much as he. He was very exemplary in his life and conversation, endeavoured at all times to perform the duties, whether public or private, which devolved on him, and whatever he did was done cheerfully, as for the glory of God.[10]

By all accounts, Miller was a humble, self-effacing man. He had no drive to promote himself. However, he was so well received in Dresden that invitations poured in for him to speak in churches and at gatherings throughout eastern New York, Vermont, and bordering areas of Canada—and in a few years, throughout lower Canada, southern Maine, Massachusetts, Rhode Island, and Pennsylvania. At the peak of the Millerite movement, he also spoke in western New York and Ohio.

Listeners always accorded Miller respectful, even excited, attention. His efforts at administration, however, earned less acclaim. Fortunately, in 1839 he attracted to the Adventist cause the ultimate helper, administrator, and organizer, the Rev. Joshua Himes, the founder of the Chardon Street Chapel in Boston. Himes was active in the abolitionist and temperance movements. He heard Miller speak and quickly swung into action as his right hand. Their complementary skills made Himes and Miller a superb team.

Himes's efforts generated a flurry of activity and then a frenzy. He started the first Millerite newspaper, *The Signs of the Times,* in Boston in 1840, first published twice-weekly and then weekly. Within seven months he had one thousand subscribers.[11] In 1842, Himes started *The Midnight Cry* in New York City with an associate, Nathaniel Southard. They distributed 240,000 copies within two weeks of its founding, and within five months half a million copies had been distributed.[12] The *Signs* and the *Cry* were the two most important Millerite papers. Other Adventist newspapers and newsletters were also founded, including *The Trumpet of Alarm* in Philadelphia, *Second Advent of Christ* in Cleveland, *Voice of Elijah* in Montreal, and *The Western Midnight Cry* in Cincinnati. More than forty such periodicals were in circulation by October 1844. Historians estimate that five million pieces of Millerite Adventist literature were disseminated by May 1844—one piece for every four men, women, and children in the United States.[13]

Miller and at least two hundred other preachers spoke in churches of many denominations, in lecture halls, and at camp meetings that were often held in large tents. Sometimes thousands of people attended a camp meeting over several days to hear from many ministers. In fact, the largest tent ever built at the time, the "big tent," was constructed in 1842 to hold four thousand people. It was then enlarged to accommodate six thousand people. A streamer bearing the words "Thy Kingdom Come" flew from the towering staff. The Millerite Adventists held at least 125 of these camp meetings throughout the Northeast, welcoming an estimated half million people. The population of the United States was about 17 million at that time, with perhaps half in the Northeast, meaning that as many as one in fifteen Northeasterners attended an Adventist camp meeting.

It is of interest that the Adventist movement that Miller reluctantly came to lead held a *premillennial* view of the

Second Coming, meaning that Jesus would *inaugurate* the thousand years of peace and justice on earth noted in prophecies. This perspective marked a split from the traditional *postmillennial* Protestant belief that Jesus would return at the end of a millennium of peace and justice that Christians would accomplish in preparation of the earth for Him.

The 1830s and '40s were a heyday for reform movements such as women's rights and abolitionism. Millerism was foremost among them because it offered the hope that Jesus would revitalize the earth and banish evil when He returned. This prospect increased the yearning of the Millerites for the Second Coming as the following hymn expresses:

> *How long, O Lord our Savior,*
> *Wilt thou remain away?*
> *Our hearts are growing weary,*
> *Of thy so long delay.*[14]

CHAPTER 2

The Prophet Daniel: 2,300 Days

Biblical scholars and lay persons alike scrutinized the entire Bible for prophetic indications of the time of the Second Coming. Perhaps none of the classical prophets of the Hebrew Bible mystified readers and generated more diverse interpretations than the enigmatic prophecies of Daniel. His visions featured inexplicable symbols—a beast with ten horns, a ram with a unicorn-like horn that turns into four horns, and an abomination that causes desolation. Then there were his numbers—the seventy sevens, the 1,260 days, the 1,290 days, the 1,335 days, and the 2,300 days. Daniel's visions have perplexed Jewish and Christian theologians from his time to ours, and the Adventists were not exempt. The book of Daniel was the last book of the prophets to be accepted into the canon of the Hebrew Bible.

According to the book of Daniel, Daniel lived from the late seventh century into the mid-sixth century BCE. He grew up in the Kingdom of Judah but was taken to Babylon as a youth. After the Assyrian Empire fell to the Babylonians in 609 BCE, the vassal Israelite state of Judah was required to pay tribute to the victors. Beyond gold, silver, and crops, that tribute included human resources. Promising young men of Judah's royal house and nobility were sent to Babylon in 605 for training as servants in the royal court. Daniel was among them.

Daniel's visions and numbers have always generated varied interpretations. Yet his clues spoke clearly to the Millerites. Consider Daniel's prophecy that the sanctuary would be cleansed in 2,300 days. Millerites believed that those 2,300 days stood for years and held the key to pinpointing the time of the return of Christ, known as the time of the end and marked by the Last Judgment and the ushering in of the Kingdom of God.

The first step to interpreting Daniel's visions was understanding the biblical numerical code for time. The Millerites knew that one day equaled one year, as these two biblical verses indicate: *"For forty years—one year for each of the forty days you explored the land—you will suffer for your sins and know what it is like to have me against you,"* (Numbers 14:34) and *"I have assigned you the same number of days as the years of their sin. So for 390 days you will bear the sin of the people of Israel."* (Ezekiel 4:5) In biblical counting, one year equals 360 days and a "time" means one year. Therefore, one time plus two times plus half a time equal three and a half years. With 360 days per year, that's a total of 1,260 biblical days, or years.

Like those of many of his colleagues and other Adventist scholars of his time, Miller's computations applied this code when interpreting a vision described in Daniel 8:1–14 in which Daniel saw himself by the Ulai Canal in Susa, in the province of Elam,[1] Persia. He saw a ram with two long horns charging west, north, and south. Next, a goat with one horn between its eyes came from the west, crossing the whole earth without touching the ground. It charged the ram in great rage, shattering the ram's two horns. The goat trampled the defeated ram and became very great, but the goat's large horn broke off at the height of its power. In its place grew four prominent horns that pointed toward the four winds of heaven. Out of one of the horns grew another, increasing in power to the south, to the east, and toward the Beautiful Land:

> It grew until it reached the host of the heavens, and it threw some of the starry host down to the earth and trampled on them. It set itself up to be as great as the commander of the army of the Lord; it took away the daily sacrifice from the Lord, and his sanctuary was thrown down. Because of rebellion, the Lord's people and the daily sacrifice were given over to it. It prospered in everything it did, and truth was thrown to the ground. (Daniel 8:10–12)

The vision continued as Daniel heard a holy one ask that eternal question, "When?"

> Then I heard a holy one speaking, and another holy one said to him, "How long will it take for the vision to be fulfilled—the vision concerning the daily sacrifice, the rebellion that causes desolation, the surrender of the sanctuary and the trampling underfoot of the Lord's people?"
>
> He said to me, "It will take 2,300 evenings and mornings; then the sanctuary will be reconsecrated." (Daniel 8:13–14)

Using the biblical numerical code, 2,300 days meant 2,300 years. But when should the counting start?

The conventional starting date, according to biblical scholars, was the edict of the Persian king Artaxerxes I to rebuild Jerusalem. By way of background, Jerusalem had been destroyed by the Babylonians in 587 BCE, and the Babylonians were subsequently defeated by the Persians under Cyrus the Great in 539. Persian kings had issued two previous decrees that allowed the rebuilding of the Temple, but the third one, issued in 457 by Artaxerxes I and given to Ezra, authorized the rebuilding of the city of Jerusalem. (Ezra 7:1, 6, 8, 11–26) The years from the third decree to the birth of Christ numbered 456. Subtracting that number from the 2,300 years in Daniel's prophecy results in 1,844 years, which led Miller and other Adventists to believe that Daniel's vision would be fulfilled in 1844 CE by the return of Jesus Christ. In that context, the cleansing of the sanctuary would be the Last Judgment, the banishment of sin from the earth.

What could possibly be more important in human affairs than the Second Coming in a few short years or months? The Millerites' flurry of activity became a frenzy of preparation.

CHAPTER 3

A Frenzy of Preparation

W as Jesus actually going to return soon? Were the end times really so close at hand? Countless people in North America and Europe believed so. An otherworldly influence was not only wafting on the breeze but raising windstorms.

In 1833, Miller published a 64-page pamphlet titled *Evidences from Scripture and History of the Second Coming of Christ About the Year 1843; and of His Personal Reign of One Thousand Years*. He maintained a constant stream of encouraging correspondence with his Adventist colleagues. For example, in a letter dated April 10, 1833, to his close friend Truman Hendryx, he wrote:

> O may the Bible be to us a rock, a pillar, a compass, a chart, a statute, a dictionary, a polar star, a traveller's guide, a pilgrim's companion, a shield of faith, a ground of hope, a history, a chronology, an armory, a store-house, a mirror, a toilet, a closet, a prayer book ...
>
> It is meat, food, drink, raiment, shelter, warmth, heat, a feast, fruit, apples, pictures, wine, milk, honey, bread butter, oil,... it teaches salvation, justification, sanctification, redemption and glorification; it

declares condemnation, destruction, and desolation; it tells us what we were, are, and shall be; begins with the beginning, carries us through the intermediate, and ends only with the end; ...[1]

Millerite literature traveled around the world. In 1836, Miller released a book of nineteen lectures, *Evidence from Scripture and History of the Second Coming of Christ About the Year 1843: Exhibited as a Course of Lectures.* From 1831 through 1843, he is estimated to have delivered 4,500 sermons and lectures in 4,000 communities before at least 500,000 people.[2]

In many instances, Miller's lectures did seem to trigger social reforms as well as to gain fervent believers. For example, after Miller lectured in Portland, Maine, between March 11 and 25, 1840, Elder L. D. Fleming, pastor of the Christian Church in that city, wrote:

> At some of our meetings, since Brother M. left, as many as two hundred and fifty, it has been estimated, have expressed a desire for religion, by coming forward for prayers; and probably between one and two hundred have professed conversion at our meetings; and now the fire is being kindled through this whole city and all the adjacent country. A number of rum-sellers have turned their shops into meeting-rooms, and those places that were once devoted to intemperance and revelry are now devoted to prayer and praise. Infidels, Deists, Universalists, and the most abandoned profligates, have been converted, – some who have not been to the house of worship for years. Prayer meetings have been established in every part of the city ... I was conducted into a

room over one of the banks, where I found about thirty or forty men, of different denominations, engaged, with one accord, in prayer, at about eleven o'clock in the daytime![3]

However, both the secular and religious press presented mixed coverage of Millerite talks and events. Miller wrote:

> In all the cities which I have visited, the editors of religious newspapers have almost invariably misstated and ridiculed my views, doctrines, and motives; but in Portland I found, as I honestly believe, an honest editor. He gave a candid, honest, and impartial account.[4]

Adverse publicity, though, sparked curiosity and brought out the crowds. Millerite literature was not only widely circulated in the northeast United States but also in Europe, especially in England. By 1844, hundreds of Church of England ministers were preaching the immediate return of Christ.

What was new about Millerism? Certainly not the belief in Christ's physical return to earth and the Last Judgment. Traditional Christianity had always taught that Christ would return after a millennium of reform, after Christians had prepared the earth for Him. The Millerite phenomenon introduced a couple of important doctrinal differences—that Christ would return *imminently* and *before* the beginning of the millennium. Miller wrote in 1822:

> I found that the only millennium taught by the word of God is the thousand years which are to intervene between the first resurrection and that of the rest of the dead, as inculcated by the twentieth

of Revelation; and that it must necessarily follow the personal coming of Christ and the regeneration of the earth:* that, till Christ's coming, and the end of the world, the righteous and the wicked are to continue together on the earth.[5]

* Revelation 20:2–7

Also new was the extraordinary excitement Millerism generated among the general population. The expectation of the Advent was essentially a movement waiting for a leader. Miller may have been divinely and gently ushered into the role because of his solid scholarship, gentle and patient character, and perseverance and faith. As time went on, he proved to be a moderating influence in a movement that was prone to schisms and fanaticism. Millerism folded together new converts with people who were already expecting the Advent, the unchurched with the churched, the rabble with the respectable. In that sense, Millerism went beyond promoting ecumenism within Christian churches to unifying people from all aspects of society.

Despite the Millerite movement's appeal in the Northeast, it never gained much traction in the southern United States. Adventist sects would later spread throughout the country, but Millerism itself was rooted in Yankee culture and religious traditions.

How many Millerites were there? That is difficult to estimate because Miller strongly advised that followers remain in their own churches, although some fell away from their churches or were ostracized within them. Sometimes their pastors became Millerites, while other pastors objected to the supernaturalism of Millerism and believed in the slow progress that would usher in the millennium. It appears that most people had been exposed to the Millerite movement by 1843 and '44, but it was not a "joiner" organization. No data was kept on the number of believers.

Who were the believers? Evidently, they came from all levels of society, all walks of life, but they also seemed to be in better financial circumstances than average. David L. Rowe reported that in 1844 sixteen families in Ithaca, New York, signed a letter avowing their faith in Adventism and twelve of these families were shown in the 1850 census, which recorded financial data. "If we take their average worth that year and compare it with a random sample of Ithacans taken from the same census, we find that the Millerites averaged nearly $200 more in worth than the average Ithacan."[6]

Millerism seems to have been received equally well in rural areas, small towns, and cities in the Northeast. "Simply put, the movement appeared in all sorts of communities—rural, commercial and commercializing, industrial and industrializing—with no clear affinity for any one."[7] Women also emerged publicly as active Millerites. "The Adventist movement allowed, although it did not encourage, women to lecture publicly on Adventism, and Adventist sources are replete with stories of wives converting husbands both to righteousness and to Adventism in the privacy of their homes. As with other revivals, Adventist meetings were family affairs, as petitions to Miller asking him to preach indicate."[8]

Millerism had wide appeal because its message was so rational and his scholarly methods so traditional. In effect, he simply took two steps beyond traditional Christian theology—the *imminence* of the Second Coming *before* the millennium. However, the emphasis on an imminent return stirred the inevitable "when?" questions.

Many Millerites, including some of Miller's closest clergy friends, placed incessant pressure on Miller to give a date for the event. Even though in 1822 Miller gave the year 1843 in his Articles of Faith as the time of the return, he took a soft approach that emphasized the *certainty* of a quickly-approaching return, *not the date*. Acquiescing to the demand for a more precise time, shortly before the beginning of 1843, Miller issued a synopsis of his views, of which Article XVI stated:

> I believe the time can be known by all who desire to understand and be ready for his coming. And I am fully convinced that some time between 21st March, 1843, and March 21st, 1844, according to the Jewish mode of computation of time, Christ will come, and bring all his saints with him; and that then he will reward every man as his works shall be. (Based on Matthew 16:27 and Revelation 22:12)[9]

The year 1843 was one of ardent expectancy. Miller sent a New Year's address to his followers dated January 1, 1843, that overflowed with joy. "This year—O blessed year!—the captive will be released, the prison doors will be opened, death will have no more dominion over us, and life, eternal life, will be our everlasting reward."[10] Coincidentally, as if to underscore the expectancy, a comet of unusual brilliance appeared in February 1843, leading many people to interpret the phenomenon as a sign of the Lord's coming.

Enthusiasm grew as the time got short. Phrases such as "if time should last" often punctuated appointments. A common greeting was "He will come." By December 1843, the Millerite newspaperman Himes planned to publish one million tracts before March 1844 and his counterparts were printing newsletters as fast as they could. Speaking work was concentrated in the larger metropolitan areas of the Northeast in order to maximize the number of people reached. As the Second Great Awakening neared its zenith, the compulsion to spread the word gripped Millerite ministers and laymen alike.

This fervent missionary activity caused churches and society at large to become increasingly divided between the believers and the nonbelievers. The more actively Millerites preached their faith, the more aggressively critics moved against them with sarcastic newspaper articles. Some Adventist properties were vandalized and hooligans occasionally caused physical violence at camp meetings. Inherent in these problems was their solution— either the Second Advent would occur, or it would not. The believers were not the only ones anxiously waiting for an end.

Of course, the press had a field day with Millerism. For example, Moses Stuart, one of the foremost biblical scholars in the 1840s, wrote with razor-edged sarcasm in the *New York Herald* after it erroneously printed April 3, 1844, as the date of the return:

> I would respectfully suggest, that in some way or other they [Miller and his followers] have in all probability made a small mistake as to the exact day of the month when the grand catastrophe takes place, the FIRST *of April* being evidently much more appropriate to their arrangements than any other day of the year.[11]

And the *Lowell Courier* also got in its licks:

> Mr. Miller has been holding forth on his narrow-minded humbug at Trenton to large audiences.

This Miller does not appear to be a knave, but simply a fool, or more properly a monomaniac. If the Almighty intended to give due notice of the world's destruction, He would not do it by sending a fat, illiterate old fellow to preach bad grammar and worse sense, down in Jersey.[12]

When the year between March 21, 1843, and March 21, 1844, came and went without the occurrence of the Advent, Miller was caught between puzzlement and disappointment. He wrote to Himes on May 2, 1844, a long letter addressed to Second Advent believers for publication in his *Advent Herald*, the new name for *The Signs of the Times*. It started as follows:

Were I to live my life over again, with the same evidence that I then had, to be honest with God and man, I should have to do as I have done.

I *confess my error*, and acknowledge *my disappointment*; yet I still believe that the day of the Lord is near, even at the door; and I exhort you, my brethren, to be watchful, and not let that day come upon you unawares. The wicked, the proud, the bigot will exult over us. I will try to be patient. God will deliver the godly out of temptation, and will reserve the unjust to be punished at Christ's appearing"[13]

Miller maintained that he would have lived his life no differently despite the disappointment. But he also expressed his inner feelings in a heart-wrenching poem:

How tedious and lonesome the hours,
While Jesus, my Saviour, delays!

I have sought him in solitude's bowers,
And looked for him all the long days.

Yet he lingers—I pray tell me why
His chariot no sooner returns?
To see him in clouds in the sky,
My soul with intensity burns.

I long to be with him at home,
My heart swallowed up in his love,
On the fields of New Eden to roam,
And to dwell with my Savior above.[14]

Many Millerites left the movement entirely after March 21, 1844, and returned to their churches if they had not been removed from the rolls. Others scrutinized the calculations for errors to determine a new date for the Advent. Had there been a problem handling a transitional year between what we now call BCE and CE? Had there been a year zero? The 1843 projections assumed so. If there was no zero year (and there was not), then the calculations actually pointed to a year later, 1844.

New theories emerged to guide the setting of a new date. One study pointed to April 18, 1844, based on the Karaite Jewish calendar[15] rather than the Rabbinic calendar, but to no avail. Scholars examined and preached the concept of *tarrying* for two or three months during the summer of 1844. After all, they suggested, Noah had to tarry a week while God gave humanity its last chance, even though the Ark was loaded and set to go. (Genesis 7:14) And the prophet Habakkuk said, *"For the vision is yet for an appointed time, but at the end it shall speak, and not lie: though it tarry, wait for it; because it will surely come, it will not tarry."* (Habakkuk 2:3 KJV) They also found solace in Hebrews 10:36–39:

For ye have need of patience, that, after ye have done the will of God, ye might receive the promise.

For yet a little while, and he that shall come will come, and will not tarry.

Now the just shall live by faith: but if any man draw back, my soul shall have no pleasure in him.

But we are not of them who draw back unto perdition; but of them that believe to the saving of the soul.

Giving credence to these efforts, most Millerites took heart and continued their mission to proclaim the imminent return of Jesus. This despite the fact that Miller was unique among leaders of mass religious movements because he lacked a charismatic personality and exciting oratorical skills and thought only of service to his Lord rather than personal gain. A pen portrait—a brief written description—was written about Miller in February 1844 by one of his friends. It offers an insightful look at his character and personality:

There is a kindness of soul, simplicity, and power, peculiarly original, combined in his manner; and he is affable and attentive to all, without any affectation of superiority. He is of about medium stature, a little corpulent, and, in temperament, a mixture of sanguine and nervous. His intellectual developments are unusually full, and we see in his head great benevolence and firmness, united with a lack of self-esteem. He is wanting in marvelousness, and is naturally skeptical. His countenance is full and round, while there is a peculiar expression in his blue eye, of shrewdness and love. Although about sixty-two years of age, his hair is not gray, but of a light, glossy autumn; his voice is full and distinct, and his pronunciation somewhat northern-antique. In his social relations, he is gentle and affectionate, and insures the esteem of all with whom he mingles. In giving this charcoal sketch to the public, I have merely sought to correct numerous misstatements, and gratify the honest desire of many honest believers with a faint outline of the character and appearance of the man.[16]

The writer presents a seemingly average man who developed his God-given intellectual capabilities despite a lack of formal education; who pursued his biblical studies in a disciplined manner; who communicated well with everyone from a modest stance; and who was driven not by ego, but by his deep desire to fulfill the command to "tell the world."

CHAPTER 4

The Great Disappointment

Renewed hope for an imminent Second Coming started gaining momentum in the summer of 1844 because of a new interpretation of the cleansing of the sanctuary in Daniel 8:14—the seven-month theory. Miller had speculated about this in 1843 but then set it aside. It fell to Samuel S. Snow, a little-known Millerite preacher, to aggressively promote it. Snow viewed the ceremonial Jewish Sabbaths as types and aspects of Jesus's ministry as anti-types. Snow believed that the spring Jewish Holy Days such as Passover, the festival of First Fruits, and the Feast of Weeks were fulfilled by Jesus, while the fall events had not yet been fulfilled. Therefore, so the reasoning went, He would return in the seventh month of 1844 on Yom Kippur, the Day of Atonement—October 22, according to the Karaite calendar. Snow preached the seventh-month interpretation at the August 1844 camp meeting held in Exeter, New Hampshire.

The August 21 issue of the *Advent Herald* reported on Snow's pronouncement in rather tepid terms. The editors reported that "Brother Snow remarks with great energy on the *time*, and displayed much research" in presenting his views. Granting that his conclusions were a possibility, the *Herald* cautioned that "we should hesitate before we should feel authorized to attempt to 'make known' the very *day*." It went on to suggest that all should examine the evidence.[1]

Snow's newspaper, the *True Midnight Cry*, that he had founded explicitly to publicize the seventh-month interpretation, released its first issue the next day on August 22. For its time, Snow's blitz of press runs and distribution could rival today's mass marketing. Snow explained:

> God is an *exact time keeper*. ... those types which were to be observed in the 7th month, have never yet had their fulfillment.
>
> The *important point* in this type is the *completion* of the reconciliation at the *coming* of the high priest *out of* the holy place. The high priest was a type of Jesus our Holy Priest; the most holy place a type of heaven itself; and the coming out of the high priest a type of the coming of Jesus the second time to bless his waiting people. As this was on the tenth day of the 7th month, so on that day Jesus will certainly come, because not a *single point* of the law is to fail. *All must be fulfilled.*[2]

Believing that the 2,300 days of Daniel 8:14 ended in 1844, Snow proclaimed that Jesus would come on "the *tenth day* of the *seventh month*" of "the *present* year,"[3] on Yom Kippur. According to the Hebrew Bible, Moses was told by God:

> *This is to be a lasting ordinance for you: On the tenth day of the seventh month you must deny yourselves and not do any work—whether native-born or a*

foreigner residing among you—because on this day atonement will be made for you, to cleanse you. Then, before the Lord, you will be clean from all your sins. It is a day of sabbath rest, and you must deny yourselves; it is a lasting ordinance. The priest who is anointed and ordained to succeed his father as high priest is to make atonement. He is to put on the sacred linen garments and make atonement for the Most Holy Place, for the tent of meeting and the altar, and for the priests and all the members of the community. (Leviticus 16:29–33)

If a year was counted from the spring solstice, Yom Kippur would occur in the fall. In the year 1844, Yom Kippur would fall on October 22 of the Gregorian calendar.

Most Millerites did not initially endorse Snow's message or his new date for the Advent even though Miller himself, more than a year earlier, had considered the same arguments. On May 17, 1843, the *Signs of the Times* had published Miller's comments that "the ceremonies of the typical law that were observed in the first month, or the vernal equinox, had their fulfillment in Christ's first advent and sufferings; but all the feasts and ceremonies of the seventh month, or autumnal equinox, can only have their fulfillment at the second advent," and Yom Kippur "is certainly typical of the atonement Christ is now making for us."[4]

Miller had not pursued these thoughts further since 1843, though. He and Himes only reluctantly endorsed the October 22, 1844, date in late September, only a few weeks before October 22. But when they did, massive printing efforts and revitalized speaking tours spread the news like proverbial wildfire.

As the apocalyptic date approached, newspapers reported that some farmers left their crops unharvested in the fields because there would be no need for them. Many Millerites sold their earthly possessions, businesses, and even farms, some for cents on the dollar. They made spiritual preparations by paying debts and making restitution for stolen property and other sins. When the date of the expected coming of their Lord arrived, they gathered in groups to sing and pray. However, any donning of white ascension robes seems to have been limited to a myth that gained veracity only through repeated telling in the ensuing years.

At long last, the longed-for day came—but it went as all other days had. The *Baltimore Sun* reported, "The Millerites ... kept it up all night before last and yesterday they went to bed—their public haunts are silent as the grave."[5] The *Cleveland Plain Dealer* summed it up this way:

> The world still hangs fire. The old planet is still on the track, notwithstanding the efforts to 'stop er.' The "believers" in this city, after being up a few nights watching and making noises like serenading tom cats, have now gone to bed and concluded to take a snooze. We hope they will wake up rational beings![6]

The non-event earned the title of the Great Disappointment. Washington Morse (1816–1909) of Northfield, Vermont, gave a poignant description of how that day came and went with its bitter disappointment.

> The day came and passed, and the darkness of another night closed in upon the world. But with that darkness came a pang of disappointment to

the advent believers that can find a parallel only in the sorrow of the disciples after the crucifixion of their Lord. The passing of the time was a bitter disappointment. True believers had given up all for Christ, and had shared His presence as never before. The love of Jesus filled every soul; and with inexpressible desire they prayed, "Come, Lord Jesus, and come quickly;" but He did not come. And now, to turn again to the cares, perplexities, and dangers of life, in full view of jeering and reviling unbelievers, who scoffed as never before, was a terrible trial of faith and patience. When Elder Himes visited Waterbury, Vt., a short time after the passing of the time and stated that the brethren should prepare for another cold winter, my feelings were almost uncontrollable. I left the place of meeting and wept like a child.[7]

Morse did not, however, lose faith. He and his wife joined the Sabbatarian (seventh-day worship) movement that would later produce the Seventh-day Adventist Church. He moved with his family to Minnesota in the late 1850s and continued his evangelistic work there.

Millerism declined as only a few of the stalwarts remained faithful and most other followers drifted into sectarian Adventism. One of the stalwarts was Himes, who continued his journeys on the circuit to counsel the disappointed not only to keep their faith but also to make provision for their material needs. *The Advent Herald* published his words of encouragement: "The brethren say everywhere that the 'Herald,' and the 'Cry,' and the cause *must* be sustained. The question is settled. . . . Be of good courage. All hands are coming to the work."[8] He continued publishing the *Advent Herald* into the 1850s. Himes served consecutively with two sectarian Adventist churches, the Evangelical Adventist and the Advent Christian. In 1876, he joined the Episcopal Church, was ordained in it, and served Episcopal missions in South Dakota until his death in 1895.

Miller continued to travel widely, giving well-attended addresses to respectful audiences. He shared his deeply held convictions about the Second Coming in talks and letters. He wrote in a letter to his close friend Himes dated November 10, 1844:

> I have been waiting and looking for the blessed hope, in expectation of realizing the glorious things which God has spoken of Zion. Yes; and although I have been twice disappointed, I am not yet cast down or discouraged. God has been with me in spirit, and has comforted me. I have now much more evidence that I do believe in God's word. My mind is perfectly calm, and my hope in the coming of Christ is as strong as ever.[9]

On December 3 of that year, the *Advent Herald* published these thoughts from Miller:

> I have never enjoyed more calmness of mind, nor more resignation to the holy will of God, and patience of spirit, than I have within a few weeks past. My *faith* is stronger than ever; and this is somewhat remarkable, when I reflect on the disappointment I have met in my former expectations. But here, too, I see the good hand of God in my strength of faith.[10]

Many Millerites did not share this view. Some faded away in disappointment or embarrassment, especially when left destitute and dependent on charity to get through the winter. Others played instrumental roles in splintering the movement into sects and radical fringe groups. Within a year, about twenty-five such sects had emerged from what had once been a united movement crossing many denominations. Adventism descended into chaos primarily because it encouraged each individual to interpret the Bible as he or she saw fit. George R. Knight, a leading historian of the Seventh-day Adventist Church, wrote:

> *Disorientation* and *disarray* are two words that help us capture the mood and structure of Millerite Adventism after October 22, 1844. Whereas once the movement had known exactly where it was going and had fair ideas of how to reach its goals, after the passing of the date, the Adventists had neither of those comforting convictions of certainty. The months and years after October 1844 catapulted the Adventists into a search for identity, a task they had never thought they would have to undertake, and one for which, in many ways, they were ill-equipped.[11]

Himes called for a conference of mainstream Millerites (then known as Second Adventists) to be held in Albany, New York, in April 1845. Its purpose was to strengthen each attendee in the truth of Adventism, to consider the best means of carrying forth Adventist work, to continue preparing Adventists for the coming of their Lord, and to convert and save sinners.

Sixty-one delegates, including Miller, attended the Albany conference. Miller submitted a long paper to the conference, called his Address to the Brethren, which the delegates adopted unanimously. Highlights from the Address include:

> The cause we advocate calls upon all men to read the word of God and to reason, judge, compare, and digest for themselves. Yet this very liberty may become a stumbling-block to many and, without charity, be the means of scattering, dividing, and causing contention among brethren.

> … we must learn to judge men and principles by their fruits. … Any man whose object is to obtain followers must be avoided. Whatever produces envy and strife, brethren, is of the devil; … Some are neglecting the lamp, and seeking to walk by sparks of their own kindling.

> Our disappointment, as to the time, should have no effect on our hope. We know that Christ has not yet been revealed, and the subject of our hope is yet in the future. Therefore, if we believe in God's word, as we profess, we ought to be thankful for the trial of our faith.[12]

Delegates sought a middle ground around the meaning of the cleansing of the sanctuary. A twelve-member committee, including Miller and Himes, was appointed to arrange the business of the conference. Committee participants strove for unity as they drew up a ten-point doctrinal platform of Adventist belief called "Important Truths." (See Appendix B) This statement of belief had no provisions for a time element for the return of Christ although it did stress that the Advent was near.

The delegates prepared a plan of action to convert people to Adventism through preaching services, literature, Sunday schools, and Bible classes. They also passed a series of resolutions. One was the rejection of postmillennialism and another was the denial that the Jews would be restored as a nation at any point in time. The Adventists resolved that they would have no fellowship with anyone who created theological obstacles to the condition of salvation, which was the acceptance of Jesus, or indulged in behaviors considered aberrant, such as communal foot washing, sitting on the floor, shaving one's head to achieve humility, and deliberately acting like children in understanding. The conference ordained five ministers and approved a statement to guide independent church congregations.

The Albany conference strengthened the moderates and rejected new and fringe movements. But the conference also inadvertently created a dividing line between the ministers and followers who adopted the Albany conference doctrines and resolutions and those who did not. Once self-study of the Bible had been endorsed, with every person independently seeking interpretations, there was no going back. Individuals were only limited by their imagination in developing new theologies and they proceeded apace. Schisms, unusual theologies, and fanaticism emerged to provide plenty of choices for disappointed Millerites. Miller, Himes, and other Millerite leaders struggled to prevail over schismatic beliefs and to maintain unity in Adventism, but the principle of self-study and individual interpretation of the Bible undermined all prospects for a unified Adventist movement. Throughout the late 1840s and 1850s, the number of Adventist sects continued to multiply. Most of them disappeared between the 1860s and the early twentieth century, following interminable debates, schisms, mergers, and collapses.

Millerism had been an ecumenical movement that crossed most Protestant denominational lines. This ecumenism collapsed when Jesus did not return as expected. Most mainstream Protestant churches turned against the Millerite influence and forced those who remained firm in Adventist belief to look for other places of worship. Miller himself, along with other believers in his hometown in Low Hampton, New York, was no longer welcome at the local Baptist church where he had worshipped, spoken, and taught Sunday school for many years.

Miller did not disavow any aspect of his faith that had developed from his biblical studies. He admitted to making errors in calculations and continued to exhort everyone to study the Bible for himself. His Address to the Public, printed in the *Advent Herald* on September 9, 1846, read in part:

> I readily confess I was misled in my calculations; not by the word of God, nor by the established principles of interpretation I adopted, but by the authorities which I followed in history and chronology, and which have been generally considered worthy of the fullest confidence.
>
> The testimony of historians, as to the dates of events, cannot affect the testimony of the word of God, that, at certain periods from these events, his promises will be fulfilled. They may fail, but his word cannot fail.

I am thankful to God, although much and severely disappointed, that I never pretended to be divinely inspired, but always directed you to the same source from which I obtained all the information I then had and now possess on this glorious and heart-cheering subject. Let me, then, exhort you, kind reader, by the value of truth, by the worth of your own soul, and the love of life everlasting, to examine your Bible on the coming of Christ, the redemption of the body, the salvation of your soul, and the everlasting inheritance. ... examine for yourselves; let no man deceive you in these days of deception, when the devil has come, deceiving, if possible, the very elect.[13]

Miller remained firm in his faith with equanimity and urged his colleagues and fellow Adventists to do the same. He spent the rest of his life repudiating splinter theories, restating his own convictions, and losing the effort to preserve unity in the Adventist movement. Approaching the end of his life, he wrote to the annual conference of Adventists that was held in Boston on May 12, 1849:

My belief is unshaken in the correctness of the conclusions I have arrived at and maintained during the last twenty years. I see no reason to question the evidence on which rest the fundamental principles of our faith. I cannot avoid the belief that the earth is to be restored to its Eden state, and become the eternal residence of the saints; that Christ is to come personally, to reign on the earth; that he will redeem us from death, and ransom us from the power of the grave; that he will change our vile bodies into the likeness of his glorified body, and destroy those who destroy the earth; and that at his coming will be the restoration of all things spoken of by the mouth of all the holy prophets since the world began, the establishment of the new heavens and new earth, the resurrection of the righteous, and the change of the living wicked from the earth—whose resurrection will not transpire until after one thousand years.[14]

Miller's health had been failing for some time. His close friend and colleague Himes visited with him from late November 1849 until his passing on December 20. The words on Miller's tombstone in the family burying ground half a mile away read: *"But go thy way till the end be, thou shalt rest, and stand in thy lot at the end of the days."* (Daniel 12:13, KJV)

Perhaps the most serious challenge faced by Millerism had been its adherents' inability to understand the full import of the prophecies of Daniel because their meanings had been sealed: *"Go your way, Daniel, because the words are rolled up and sealed until the time of the end."* (Daniel 12:9) It was one thing to calculate numbers and interpret events that seemed like those that Jesus warned would precede His return, but scripture itself explained that the prophecies of Daniel would not be unsealed until *after* the time of the end, *after* the return.

In addition, the Millerite movement seems to have disregarded the words of Jesus Himself when asked the "when?" question: *"But about that day or hour no one knows, not even the angels in heaven, nor the Son, but only the Father. As it was in the days of Noah, so it will be at the coming of the Son of Man."* (Matthew 24:36–37)

The people of Noah's time were busy living their lives as people are now. They were also oblivious to the Prophet in their midst. Then the flood came.

With the gift of hindsight, it may be easy to mock or denigrate Millerism. But that does not answer the larger question: Was there really something in the air, of which just a whiff was intoxicating? Was there indeed to be a "return," but perhaps not as Christians expected? Could the meaning of the "return" have been something other than the appearance of the physical Jesus? And most importantly, had Millerism inadvertently advanced the right year but on the wrong continent?

Unknown to the Millerites, Shia Muslims in the East, in Iraq and Persia, were living in a parallel state of expectancy for the imminent return of the Qa'im, the Risen One, the long-hidden twelfth Imam.

CHAPTER 5

Expectancy in the East

To understand the expectation of a divine coming that was stirring among Shia Muslims in the Middle East—and the importance of the twelve Imams—one must be aware of the events that split Islam into its Sunni and Shia factions immediately after Muhammad's death in 632 CE.

There is a Shia *hadith*,[1] or tradition, that in the last year of His life, Muhammad announced to His followers that His designated successor was His cousin, 'Alí-ibn-i-Abi Talib, who was also His son-in-law and first disciple. Muhammad made a pilgrimage to Mecca three months before His death to give a farewell address reviewing His basic teachings. After Muhammad and His party commenced the trip home, He was taken with a sudden urge to stop and address the company of Muslims who were with Him. H. M. Balyuzi, a Baha'i scholar of Islamic history, wrote:

> Shí'ah tradition has it that on the way back to Medina, at urgent bidding received from God, Muhammad made, all of a sudden, a forced halt by the pool of Khum, a most inconvenient place; had a pulpit raised with saddles, and from this announced 'Alí as His successor, requiring the

large body of Muslims who were with Him to pledge their loyalty to 'Alí. One can look in vain in other resources for any reference to this episode, which looms large in the writings of the Shi'ahs. They preserve total silence.[2]

Shia tradition also holds that on His deathbed, Muhammad asked for writing materials so that He might dictate His last wishes. Balyuzi explained:

There seems to be some agreement that one day towards the end, Muhammad asked for writing material to be brought, so that He might dictate His last wishes. What exactly happened next is obscured by disputation. Obviously the Prophet was in extremity, because Shi'ah tradition holds that 'Umar said: "The man is delirious, the Book of God sufficeth us." It is also claimed that after 'Umar's intervention there was such a clamour in the sickroom that Muhammad told everyone to leave at once. The question arises, if the Prophet had, by the pool of Khum, appointed 'Alí as His successor and told His followers present to pledge loyalty to 'Alí, what need was there for Him to dictate His last wishes?[3]

The day after Muhammad's death, His followers chose Abu-Bakr (632–34), one of His close associates, to be the first Caliph (leader), thus passing over 'Alí. This action constituted the breaking of the Covenant between Muhammad and His followers and the violation of that Covenant caused the split of Islam into the Sunni and Shia sects. To this day, Sunni Muslims recognize the line of Muhammad's successors, whom they called Caliphs, as starting with Abu-Bakr. Shia Muslims recognize the line of Muhammad's successors, whom they call Imams, as starting with 'Alí. He was the first Imam to the Shias and the fourth Caliph to Sunnis. Had the successorship gone immediately to 'Alí in accordance with Muhammad's declaration, Islam might have had time to mature internally before extending beyond Arabia. Instead, within a year of Muhammad's passing, Abu-Bakr took Islam down the road of military conquest into bordering areas of the declining Roman and Sasanid Persian empires. The second Caliph, Umar (634–44), continued with the conquest of Antioch, Alexandria, and Jerusalem. The third Caliph, Uthman (644–56), continued military conquests that expanded the Muslim Empire to present-day Armenia, Georgia, Azerbaijan, Iran, and parts of Afghanistan, the Levant area bordering the eastern Mediterranean Sea, and North Africa from Egypt to present-day Tunisia. Waves of conversions swept through these lands with some people converting as a pragmatic way to acquiesce to life under the conquerors, but others responding to the spiritual springtime that attracts many hearts to a new Dispensation from God. Muhammad had forbidden forced conversions. He had decreed that Christians and Jews be recognized as people of the Book—those who adhered to Dispensations preceding His own and mentioned in the Qur'an. They were to receive full liberty in exchange for payment of a small annual sum.

A Prophet of God speaks for God, and violating a Prophet's directives brings dire consequences not only to the individual perpetrators but also to the people at large. The consequences of breaking the Covenant of Muhammad, the Prophet's successorship, have been felt for centuries and still reverberate throughout the Islamic world today.

Three caliphs—Abu-Bakr, Umar, and Uthman—ruled from 632 to 656. 'Alí (656–61) was finally chosen to head the Islamic Faith in 656, twenty-four years after he should have succeeded Muhammad. But it was too late for 'Alí to steer Islam as Muhammad would have wanted. He was assassinated while praying after just five years.

The introduction to the preeminent work of Baha'i history, *The Dawn-Breakers: Nabíl's Narrative of the Early Days of the Baha'i Revelation*, sets out the distinguishing features of Shia Islam:

> The cardinal point wherein the Shí'ahs (as well as the other sects included under the more general term of Imámites) differ from the Sunnís is the doctrine of the Imámate. According to the belief of the latter, the viceregency of the Prophet (Khilafat) is a matter to be determined by the choice and election of his followers, and the visible head of the Musulmán world is qualified for the lofty position which he holds less by any special divine grace than by a combination of orthodoxy and administrative capacity. According to the Imámite view, on the other hand, the viceregency is a matter altogether spiritual; an office conferred by God alone, first by His Prophet, and afterwards by those who so succeeded him, and having nothing to do with the popular choice or approval. In a word, the Khalífih of the Sunnís is merely the outward and visible Defender of the Faith: the Imám of the Shí'ahs is the divinely ordained successor of the Prophet, one endowed with all perfections and spiritual

gifts, one whom all the faithful must obey, whose decision is absolute and final, whose wisdom is superhuman, and whose words are authoritative. The general term Imámate is applicable to all who hold this latter view without reference to the way in which they trace the succession, and therefore includes such sects as the Báqirís and Ismá'ílís as well as the Shí'ahs or "Church of the Twelve" (Madhhab-i-Ithná-'Asharíyyih), as they are more specifically termed, with whom alone we are here concerned. According to these, twelve persons successively held the office of Imám. These twelve are as follows:

1. 'Alí-ibn-i-Abí-Tálib, the cousin and first disciple of the Prophet, assassinated by Ibn-i-Muljam at Kúfih, A.H. 40 (A.D. 661).

2. Hasan, son of 'Alí and Fátimih, born A.H. 2, poisoned by order of Mu'áviyih I, A.H. 50 (A.D. 670).

3. Husayn, son of 'Alí and Fátimih, born A.H. 4, killed at Karbilá on Muharram 10, A.H. 61 (Oct. 10, A.D. 680).

4. 'Alí, son of Husayn and Shahribánú (daughter of Yazdigird, the last Sásáníyán king), generally called Imám Zaynu'l-'Ábidin, poisoned by Valíd.

5. Muhammad-Báqir, son of the above-mentioned Zaynu'l-'Ábidin and his cousin Umm-i-'Abdu'lláh, the daughter of Imám Hasan, poisoned by Ibráhim ibn-i-Valíd.

6. Ja'far-i-Sádiq, son of Imám Muhammad-Báqir, poisoned by order of Mansur, the Abbáside Khalífih.

7. Músá-Kázim, son of Imám Ja'far-i-Sádiq, born A.H. 129, poisoned by order of Hárúnu'r-Ráshid, A.H. 183.

8. 'Alí-ibn-i-Músa'r-Ridá, generally called Imám Ridá, born A.H. 153, poisoned near Tús, in Khúrásan, by order of the Khalífih Ma'mun, A.H. 203, and buried at Mashad, which derives its name and its sanctity from him.

9. Muhammad-Taqí, son of Ja'far-i-Sádiq, born A.H. 195, poisoned by the Khalífih Mu'tasim at Baádad [Baghdad], A.H. 220.

10. 'Alí-Naqí, son of Imám Muhammad-Taqí, born A.H. 213, poisoned at Surra-man-Ra'á, A.H. 254.

11. Hasan-i-'Askarí, son of Imám 'Alí-Naqí, born A.H. 232, poisoned A.H. 260.

12. Muhammad, son of Imám Hasan-i-'Askarí and Nargis-Khátún, called by the Shi'ahs 'Imám-Mihdí, 'Hujjatu'lláh (the Proof of God), 'Baqíyyatu'lláh (the Remnant of God), and 'Qá'im-i-Al-i-Muhammad (He who shall arise of the family of Muhammad). He bore not only the same name but the same kunyih—Abu'l-Qásim—as the Prophet, and according to the Shi'ahs it is not lawful for any other to bear this name and this kunyih together. He was born at Surra-man-Ra'á,

A.H. 255, and succeeded his father in the Imamate, A.H. 260.

The Shi'ahs hold that he did not die, but disappeared in an underground passage in Surra-man-Ra'á, A.H. 329; that he still lives, surrounded by a chosen band of his followers, in one of those mysterious cities, Jábulqá and Jábulsá; and that when the fullness of time is come, when the earth is filled with injustice, and the faithful are plunged in despair, he will come forth, heralded by Jesus Christ, overthrow the infidels, establish universal peace and justice, and inaugurate a millennium of blessedness.[4]

Sunni Muslims hold a similar belief in the coming of the Mahdi, also called the Qa'im, a messianic redeemer of Islam who will appear on earth for a time to bring in the Day of Judgment and rid the world of evil. The Arabic *al-Mahdi* means "The Guided One" and is not mentioned in the Qur'an but only in hadiths, which have varying interpretations. The broad belief is that the Mahdi will be a descendant of Muhammad, will bring the Day of Judgment, and will redeem Islam—and that, at some point, Jesus will return to assist him. The advent of the Mahdi will be preceded by dire cosmic events, wars, turmoil, and false prophets.

Shia Islam expects the literal return of the twelfth Imam after his wait in hiding, or occultation, for many centuries. The conditions preceding the coming are similar to those expected by Sunnis: chaos, wars, corruption, and catastrophes. Shias believe that the twelfth Imam will bring the Day of Judgment, redeem Islam, and usher in an era of peace and universal reformation.

In the same way that the Millerites expected the return of Christ to be premillennial—preceding the time of peace on earth—both the Shia and Sunni expectations of the return of the twelfth Imam and the coming of the Mahdi, respectively, are also premillennial. However, Shia Islam puts far more emphasis on the end days and the Day of Judgment than does Sunni Islam.

In the early nineteenth century, schools of expectancy arose among certain Shia Muslims awaiting the imminent return of the twelfth Imam. Shia hadith offered many clues as to the nature and time of this occurrence. Searchers set out quietly to find the Qa'im, aware of the mainstream Shia clergy's vehement opposition to anything that might threaten their livelihoods or status in society. When a new Manifestation of God appears, the leaders of the previous Dispensation usually fear the loss of their financial and social positions. Clergy therefore usually react strongly against any religious or social movement that threatens their privileges.

CHAPTER 6

The Search in the East

Note: Much information in this chapter and the next two is drawn from the extensive historical account The Dawn-Breakers: Nabíl's Narrative of the Early Days of the Baha'i Revelation *written by Nabil-i-A'zam (1831–1892), who participated in many of the episodes depicted in* The Dawn-Breakers. *He also obtained first-hand accounts from many survivors of the persecutions, including Mirza Musa, the half-brother of Bahá'u'lláh, the Prophet of the Baha'i Faith. Bahá'u'lláh and 'Abdu'l-Bahá read and approved parts of the manuscript[1] and Shoghi Effendi advised that this book was an "unchallengeable textbook."[2] Readers are urged to follow the flow of events rather than become distracted by the Persian names.*

The East and the West in the nineteenth century were at opposite ends of many spectrums. Millerism developed in a society that was largely literate and where religious freedom was legally protected. There were diverse populations of Catholics, Protestants, and Jews. The predominant Protestant population encompassed innumerable denominations, sects, and theologies. Most important, North America was young and vibrant, a land of opportunity and forward thinking. Journalists could ridicule Millerism but, for the most part, believers in new and different beliefs were spared severe or overt persecution—a distinct exception being the early Mormons.

Persia was the opposite. The ancient Persian culture had fallen from its previous glory into the depths of inertia and corruption. Most people were illiterate. Women were seldom educated and almost never left their homes. In fact, men even argued about whether women had souls. The Shah of Persia was an absolute ruler who appointed all government officials and could order anyone's destiny or death. He controlled all the nation's resources. Lord George Curzon (1859–1925), a traveler, politician, and writer who spent six months in Persia in 1899 as a correspondent for the *London Times*, wrote: "In theory the king may do as he pleases; his word is law. In his person are fused the threefold functions of government, legislative, executive, and judicial. He is the pivot upon which turns the entire machinery of public life."[3]

Shia Islam prevailed in a culture where the concept of religious freedom differed markedly from the western version. Jews and Christians were granted certain protections as people of the Book, but it was heresy punishable by death for a Muslim to leave Islam for another religion. Islamic law, based on the Qur'an and hadith, ruled all aspects of Persian society, and a system of Islamic courts and councils enforced religious law. In that environment, students curious about the search for the Promised One, the Qa'im, pursued their interest cautiously.

Shaykh Ahmad

In Shia Islam, the expectancy was not associated with the prophecies of Daniel as it was in Christianity. However, the year 1844 was one thousand lunar years after the twelfth imam was believed to have entered occultation. That was considered important. A few spiritually attuned individuals interpreted allegorical references in Islamic Scripture as indications of a new divine Revelation and their intuition led them to believe that the day of its advent was near. One of these people was Shaykh Ahmad-i-Ahsa'i[4] (1753–1826), who was born in today's Bahrain. Nabil-i-A'zam described the Shaykh's awakening to his unique mission as follows:

> At a time when the shining reality of the Faith of Muhammad had been obscured by the ignorance, the fanaticism, and perversity of the contending sects into which it had fallen, there appeared above the horizon of the East that luminous Star of Divine guidance, Shaykh Ahmad-i-Ahsá'í. He observed how those who professed the Faith of Islam had shattered its unity, sapped its force, perverted its purpose, and degraded its holy name. His soul was filled with anguish at the sight of the corruption and strife which characterised the shi'ah sect of Islam. Inspired by the light that shone within him, he arose with unerring vision, with fixed purpose, and sublime detachment to utter his protest against the betrayal of the Faith by that ignoble people. Aglow with zeal and conscious of the sublimity of his calling, he vehemently appealed not only to shi'ah Islam but to all the followers of Muhammad throughout the East, to awaken from the slumber

of negligence and to prepare the way for Him who must needs be made manifest in the fulness of time, whose light alone could dissipate the mists of prejudice and ignorance which had enveloped that Faith.[5]

At age forty, in about 1793, Shaykh Ahmad felt compelled to journey to what is today called Iraq, especially to the cities of Karbila and Najaf. He was a highly educated Muslim cleric and recognized as a *mujtahid*, an authorized expounder of Islamic holy writings, and he attracted a large following. In those times, Muslim men customarily pursued their religious education by attending sessions with a mujtahid who commented on Qur'anic verses and conducted endless discourses about them. Unlike most mujtahids, however, Shaykh Ahmad was humble and mild. He believed that he must gently prepare men's hearts for the return of the twelfth Imam, although he could not openly speak of the event. However, contrary to Islamic thought and tradition, he was certain that this holy being would not come to redeem Islam:

There burned in his soul the conviction that no reform, however drastic, within the Faith of Islám, could achieve the regeneration of this perverse people. He knew, and was destined by the Will of God to demonstrate that nothing short of a new and independent Revelation, as attested and foreshadowed by the sacred Scriptures of Islám, could revive the fortunes and restore the purity of that decadent Faith.[6] *

* "He [Shaykh Ahmad] knew full well that he was chosen of God to prepare men's hearts for the reception of the more

complete truth shortly to be revealed, and that through him the way of access to the hidden twelfth Imam Mihdí was reopened. But he did not set this forth in clear and unmistakable terms, lest the 'unregenerate' should turn again and rend him." (Dr. T. K. Cheyne's "The Reconciliation of Races and Religions," p. 15.)

Intuitively, Shaykh Ahmad tapped into the concept of the divine springtime, the time when a new Prophet comes with a newly revealed Dispensation from God. Just as the phenomenal world experiences the annual cycle of spring, summer, fall, and winter, so too does the religion that emerges from the outpouring of guidance in every Divine Revelation. (See Chapter 10). Consider how 'Abdu'l-Bahá explained the spiritual seasons in a talk he gave on April 13, 1912, in New York City during his historic tour of Europe, the United States, and Canada:

> The spiritual world is like unto the phenomenal world. They are the exact counterpart of each other. Whatever objects appear in this world of existence are the outer pictures of the world of heaven. When we look upon the phenomenal world, we perceive that it is divided into four seasons; one is the season of spring, another the season of summer, another autumn and then these three seasons are followed by winter. When the season of spring appears in the arena of existence, the whole world is rejuvenated and finds new life. The soul-refreshing breeze is wafted from every direction; the soul-quickening bounty is everywhere; the cloud of mercy showers down its rain, and the sun shines upon everything. Day by day we perceive that the signs of vegetation are all about us. Wonderful flowers, hyacinths and roses perfume the nostrils. The trees are full of

leaves and blossoms, and the blossoms are followed by fruit. The spring and summer are followed by autumn and winter. The flowers wither and are no more; the leaves turn gray and life has gone. Then comes springtime; the former springtime is renewed; again a new life stirs within everything.

The appearances of the Manifestations of God are the divine springtime. When Christ appeared in this world, it was like the vernal bounty; the outpouring descended; the effulgences of the Merciful encircled all things; the human world found new life. Even the physical world partook of it. The divine perfections were upraised; souls were trained in the school of heaven so that all grades of human existence received life and light. Then by degrees these fragrances of heaven were discontinued; the season of winter came upon the world; the beauties of spring vanished; the excellences and perfections passed away; the lights and quickening were no longer evident; the phenomenal world and its materialities conquered everything; the spiritualities of life were lost; the world of existence became life unto a lifeless body; there was no trace of the spring left.[7]

The cycle of spiritual seasons has been repeated over and over. In springtime, the Prophet reiterates the eternal spiritual verities given before and adds to them in accordance with humanity's increased capacity. Old social laws are abrogated and new ones are inaugurated, not only to meet the needs of the times but also to reinforce spiritual understanding of the new religion. The people prosper for decades or centuries, experiencing the blessings of summer and the fruition of the divine Revelation. Inexorably, autumn and winter follow. Moral vitality wanes and religious and clerical corruption sets in. Memories of the spiritual fragrances, the true teachings of the founding Prophet, fade and are often lost.

Shaykh Ahmad recognized that Islam, in its turn and like every previous revelatory religion, had declined into its inevitable winter.

After several years in Iraq "and inhaling the fragrance which wafted upon him from Persia, he felt in his heart an irrepressible yearning to hasten to that country."[8] He had not yet, though, found anyone with whom he could share his innermost convictions. He would search zealously in Persia for disciples who would be open to his most important teaching.

In the early nineteenth century, Shaykh Ahmad first visited the city of Shiraz in Persia and praised it as Nabil-i-A'zam described:

> How often and how passionately he extolled that city! Such was the praise he lavished upon it that his hearers, who were only too familiar with its mediocrity, were astonished at the tone of his language. "Wonder not," he said to those who were surprised, "for ere long the secret of my words will be made manifest to you. Among you there shall be a number who will live to behold the glory of a Day which the prophets of old have yearned to witness."[9]

Mírzá 'Alí-Muhammad (the Báb) was born in Shiraz in 1819. The city was located in southwest Persia, which had once been the Babylonian province of Elam. The prophet Daniel saw himself in Susa in the province of

Elam (Daniel 8:2) when he was told about the 2,300 days (Daniel 8:14).

When Shaykh Ahmad was in Tehran in 1817, he felt a similar urgency come upon him from Nur, located north of that city. Mirza Buzurg, a well-regarded minister in the court of the Shah, had a country home in Nur where his son, Mírzá Husayn-'Alí Núrí, later known as Bahá'u'lláh, was born on November 22, 1817.

As was his pattern, Shaykh Ahmad taught his lessons in cities throughout Persia, but he seldom shared his inner thoughts until finally, in the city of Yazd, he attracted a disciple with whom he could share everything. Siyyid Kazim-i-Rashti[10] was exceedingly well educated in Islamic scriptures and, far more importantly, was attuned to higher spiritual thought. Siyyid Kazim immediately recognized the truth of Shaykh Ahmad's teaching about the fulfillment of time and the holy appearance. After a few weeks, Shaykh Ahmad left his disciples in Yazd in the care of Siyyid Kazim and continued on his travels.

In his last years, Shaykh Ahmad gave a special measure of attention to his most promising disciples so that they would recognize the events to come and support the new Revelation. He wrote books and epistles expounding on veiled Qur'anic and hadith references to that day. He spoke much—and obliquely—about 'Ali, meaning not 'Ali, the first Imam, but 'Ali-Muhammad of Shiraz (the Báb), and about Husayn, meaning not the third Imam, Husayn, but Mirzá Husayn-'Ali (Bahá'u'lláh), whose birth he had intuited in Nur.

Shaykh Ahmad and Siyyid Kazim met from time to time as the shaykh further groomed his successor. Their last meeting was in Karbila shortly before the aged shaykh left for Mecca. Nabil-i-A'zam recorded the last counsel Shaykh Ahmad imparted to Siyyid Kazim this way:

"You have no time to lose," were the last words which he addressed to him. "Every fleeting hour should be fully and wisely utilised. You should gird up the loin of endeavour and strive day and night to rend asunder, by the grace of God and by the hand of wisdom and loving-kindness, those veils of heedlessness that have blinded the eyes of men. For verily I say, the Hour is drawing nigh, the Hour I have besought God to spare me from witnessing, for the earthquake of the Last Hour will be tremendous. You should pray to God to be spared the overpowering trials of that Day, for neither of us is capable of withstanding its sweeping force. Others, of greater endurance and power, have been destined to bear this stupendous weight, men whose hearts are sanctified from all earthly things, and whose strength is reinforced by the potency of His power."[11]

Shaykh Ahmad died soon afterwards. His followers buried his body in the Cemetery Baqi, close to the tomb of Muhammad in Medina.

Siyyid Kazim

Siyyid Kazim (1793–1843) continued in Shaykh Ahmad's footsteps, earning his living as a mujtahid throughout Iraq and Persia while seeking to attract students who were receptive to the knowledge that the coming of the Promised One was near. Nabil-i-A'zam recorded:

In those days Siyyid Kázim became increasingly aware of the approach of the Hour at which the

Promised One was to be revealed. He realised how dense were those veils that hindered the seekers from apprehending the glory of the concealed Manifestation. He accordingly exerted his utmost endeavour to remove gradually, with caution and wisdom, whatever barriers might stand in the way of the full recognition of that Hidden Treasure of God. He repeatedly urged his disciples to bear in mind the fact that He whose advent they were expecting would appear neither from Jábulqá nor from Jábulsá. He even hinted at His presence in their very midst. "You behold Him with your own eyes," he often observed, "but yet recognize Him not."[12]

Siyyid Kazim suffered much hardship and persecution during his ministry. If the Shia world was waiting for the wondrous day of return foretold in Qur'anic texts and traditions, why did the intimations that this day was near arouse such hostility? The short answer is that the role of the existing clergy would be eclipsed by the Promised One. Lord Curzon observed:

Marvelously adapted alike to the climate, character, and occupations of those countries upon which it has laid its adamantine grip, Islám holds its votary in complete thrall from the cradle to the grave. To him, it is not only religion, it is government, philosophy, and science as well. The Muhammadan conception is not so much that of a state church as, if the phrase may be permitted, of a church state. The undergirders with which society itself is warped round are not of civil, but of ecclesiastical, fabrication; and, wrapped in this superb, if paralysing, creed, the Musulman lives in contented surrender of all volition, deems it his highest duty to worship God and to compel, or, where impossible, to despise those who do not worship Him in the spirit, and then dies in sure and certain hope of Paradise.[13]

The Islamic clergy wanted no changes from the corrupt status quo that ensured their livelihood, status, and power. They permitted no upsets to their lucrative, privileged systems. And most of the illiterate, poverty-stricken masses followed whatever the clergy decreed.

Little did they know that the Qa'im already walked among them, although the time had not yet come for the Promised One to declare Himself. Still, Siyyid Kazim, that venerated teacher, met and undoubtedly recognized Him at least twice. The first event occurred in Karbila when Siyyid Kazim and a small group of disciples went to visit a highly esteemed visitor to the city, a young merchant named 'Alí Muhammad-i-Shírází, who would be later known as the Báb. Among the group was his friend and confidant Shaykh Hasan-i-Zunzi, who gave Nabil-i-A'zam the following account of a remarkable meeting:

We soon reached a house, at the door of which stood a Youth, as if expectant to receive us. He wore a green turban, and His countenance revealed an expression of humility and kindliness which I can never describe. He quietly approached us, extended His arms towards Siyyid Kázim, and lovingly embraced him. His affability and loving-kindness singularly contrasted with the sense of profound reverence that characterised the attitude of Siyyid Kázim towards him. Speechless and with bowed head, he received the many expressions of affection and esteem with which that Youth greeted him. We were soon led by Him to the upper floor of that house, and entered a chamber bedecked with flowers and redolent of the loveliest perfume. He bade us be seated. We observed a silver cup which had been placed in the centre of the room, which our youthful Host, soon after we were seated, filled to overflowing, and handed to Siyyid Kázim, saying: "A drink of a pure beverage shall their Lord give them."* Siyyid Kázim held the cup with both hands and quaffed it. A feeling of reverent joy filled his being, a feeling which he could not suppress. I too was presented with a cupful of that beverage, although no words were spoken. All that was spoken at that memorable gathering was the above-mentioned verse of the Qur'an. Soon after, the host arose from his seat and, accompanying us to the threshold of his house, bade us farewell. I was mute with wonder, and knew not how to express the cordiality of His welcome, the dignity of His bearing, the charm of that face, and the delicious fragrance of that beverage. How great was my amazement when I saw my teacher quaff without the least hesitation that holy draught from a silver cup, the use of which, according to the precepts of Islám, is forbidden to the faithful. I could not explain the motive which could have induced the Siyyid to manifest such profound reverence in the presence of that Youth.[14]

*Qur'an 76:21

Three days later, Shaykh Hasan saw that same Youth arrive and take His seat among the assembled disciples of Siyyid Kazim:

He sat close to the threshold, and with the same modesty and dignity of bearing listened to the discourse of the Siyyid. As soon as his eyes fell upon that Youth, the Siyyid discontinued his address and held his peace. Whereupon one of his disciples begged him to resume the argument which he had left unfinished. "What more shall I say?" replied Siyyid Kázim, as he turned his face toward the Báb [Mírzá 'Alí-Muhammad]. "Lo, the Truth is more manifest than the ray of light that has fallen upon that lap!" I immediately observed that the ray to which the Siyyid referred had fallen upon the lap of that same Youth whom we had recently visited.[15]

The same questioner asked Siyyid Kazim why did he not reveal the name of the Promised One or identify His person:

To this the Siyyid replied by pointing with his finger to his own throat, implying that were he to divulge His name, they both would be put to death instantly. This added still further to my perplexity. I had already heard my teacher observe that so great is the perversity of this generation, that were he to point with his finger to the Promised One and say: "He indeed is the Beloved, the Desire of your hearts and mine," they would still fail to recognise and acknowledge Him. I saw the Siyyid actually point out with his finger the ray of light that had fallen on that lap, and yet none among those who were present seemed to apprehend its meaning. I, for my part, was convinced that the Siyyid himself could never be the promised One, but that a mystery inscrutable to us all lay concealed in that strange and attractive Youth.[16]

Shortly before he passed away on December 31, 1843, Siyyid Kazim exhorted his band of earnest and devoted disciples to set out on a quest for the Qa'im. The Siyyid's body was interred within the grounds of the shrine of the Imam Husayn in Karbila. Less than five months later, Mírzá 'Alí-Muhammad would reveal his identity as the Promised One to the Siyyid's foremost disciple, Mulla Husayn.

CHAPTER 7

1844 Fulfilled

Siyyid Kazim's disciples were disheartened by his death and fearful of renewed persecution at the hands of his enemies. Mulla Husayn, who had been absent on a trip when Siyyid Kazim passed away, tried to console them upon his return and to reinvigorate their spirit for the search. He asked the most distinguished and trusted of the disciples for Siyyid Kazim's expressed wishes and exhortations:

> They told him that repeatedly and emphatically, Siyyid Kázim had bidden them quit their homes, scatter far and wide, purge their hearts from every idle desire, and dedicate themselves to the quest of Him to whose advent he had so often alluded. "He told us," they said, "that the Object of our quest was now revealed. The veils that had intervened between you and Him are such that only you can remove by your devoted search. Nothing short of prayerful endeavour, of purity of motive, of singleness of mind, will enable you to tear them asunder. Has not God revealed in His Book: 'Whoso maketh efforts for Us, in Our ways will We guide them'?"* [1]
>
> * Qur'an 29:69

Mulla Husayn heeded those directives steadfastly. After forty days of prayer and meditation, he set forth for Karbila in Iraq and Bushehr in Persia, accompanied by his brother and nephew. As the men traveled, he felt pulled like a magnet to Shiraz. When they arrived outside the city, he asked his companions to proceed to a mosque and wait for him to join them.

As Mulla Husayn approached the gate in the wall around Shiraz, "his eyes fell suddenly upon a Youth of radiant countenance, who wore a green turban and who, advancing towards him, greeted him with a smile of loving welcome. He embraced Mulla Husayn with tender affection as though he had been his intimate and lifelong friend."[2] Mulla Husayn accepted the Youth's insistent invitation to visit His home, where they prayed together and where Mulla Husayn breathed an inward prayer: "I have striven with all my soul, O my God, and until now I have failed to find Thy promised Messenger. I testify that Thy word faileth not, and that Thy promise is sure."[3]

His host asked about his mission to find the promised Beloved, including what distinguishing features Siyyid Kazim had provided to help him recognize the Promised One. Mulla Husayn replied:

He is of a pure lineage, is of illustrious descent, and of the seed of Fátimih. As to His age, He is more than twenty and less than thirty. He is endowed with innate knowledge. He is of medium height, abstains from smoking, and is free from bodily deficiency.[4]

The Youth responded: *"Behold, all these signs are manifest in Me!"*[5] He went on to demonstrate that each and all applied to His person. In response, a surprised Mulla Husayn politely observed:

> He whose advent we await is a Man of unsurpassed holiness, and the Cause He is to reveal, a Cause of tremendous power. Many and diverse are the requirements which He who claims to be its visible embodiment must needs fulfil. How often has Siyyid Kázim referred to the vastness of the knowledge of the promised One! How often did he say: "My own knowledge is but a drop compared with that with which He has been endowed. All my attainments are but a speck of dust in the face of the immensity of His knowledge. Nay, immeasurable is the difference!"[6]

No sooner had Mulla Husayn spoken these words than fear and remorse seized him. Silently, he bitterly reproved himself and resolved to speak with humility. When he first started his quest, he had set two standards for ascertaining the truth about anyone who might claim to be the Qa'im. First, he would ask the person to comment on a treatise he had composed about the abstruse teachings of Shaykh Ahmad and Siyyid Kazim. Then, if the person unraveled the mysterious allusions, Mulla Husayn would ask for a commentary on the Surih[7] of Joseph from the Qur'an—a commentary he expected to be delivered without the least hesitation or reflection and in a style and language entirely different from the prevailing standards of the time. Siyyid Kazim had refused to write such a commentary, saying it was beyond him, but that "He, that great One, who comes after me will, unasked, reveal it for you. That commentary will constitute one of the weightiest testimonies of His truth, and one of the clearest evidences of the loftiness of His position."[8]

Mulla Husayn posed his first request to the Youth, who unraveled all the mysteries and solved the problems in the treatise within just a few minutes. He even surpassed Mulla Husayn's expectations by expounding on truths that could not be found in the reported sayings of the Islamic imams or in the writings of Shaykh Ahmad and Siyyid Kazim. Then He observed that had Mulla Husayn not been His guest, *"your position would indeed have been a grievous one. The all-encompassing grace of God has saved you. It is for God to test His servants, and not for His servants to judge Him in accordance with their deficient standards."*[9] Before Mulla Husayn could utter his second request, the Youth declared that it was time to reveal his commentary on the Surih of Joseph:

> He took up His pen and with incredible rapidity revealed the entire Súrih of Mulk [Dominion], the first chapter of His commentary on the Súrih of Joseph. The overpowering effect of the manner in which He wrote was heightened by the gentle intonation of His voice which accompanied His writing. Not for one moment did He interrupt the flow of the verses which streamed from His pen. Not once did He pause till the Súrih of Mulk was finished.[10]

In the company of that Youth, Mulla Husayn spent the evening and wee hours of the morning in a state of ecstasy, enthralled by the voice that rose and fell while his Host chanted the verses. The Youth told him: *"O thou who art the first to believe in Me! Verily I say, I am the Báb, the Gate of God, and thou art the Bábu'l-Báb, the gate of that Gate."*[11]

Their encounter had begun on the evening of May 22, 1844, and Mulla Husayn left the house in the early morning hours of May 23.[12]

The ministry of the Báb lasted six years from His declaration to Mulla Husayn in May 1844 until His execution in July 1850. His teachings had two major purposes—to make a sharp break from Islam, and to prepare His followers for the coming of *"Him Whom God will make manifest."* In other words, He delivered a new, independent Revelation and He also served as the herald of Bahá'u'lláh, who would bring His own Revelation. Shoghi Effendi quoted Bahá'u'lláh, and 'Abdu'l-Bahá at length on the names and identity of the Báb in poetic, mystical, and allegorical terms, as well as in decisive, clear descriptions:

> *"Essence of Essences,"* the *"Sea of Seas,"* the *"Point round Whom the realities of the Prophets and Messengers revolve,"* *"from Whom God hath caused to proceed the knowledge of all that was and shall be,"* Whose *"rank excelleth that of all the Prophets,"* and Whose *"Revelation transcendeth the comprehension and understanding of all their chosen ones,"* had delivered His Message and discharged His mission. He Who was, in the words of 'Abdu'l-Bahá, the *"Morn of Truth"* and *"Harbinger of the Most Great Light,"** Whose advent at once signalized the termination of the *"Prophetic Cycle"* and the inception of the *"Cycle of Fulfillment,"* had simultaneously through His Revelation banished the shades of night that had descended upon His country, and proclaimed the impending rise of that Incomparable Orb Whose radiance was to envelop the whole of mankind.** He, as affirmed by Himself,

"the Primal Point from which have been generated all created things," "one of the sustaining pillars of the Primal Word of God," the *"Mystic Fane,"* the *"Great Announcement,"* the *"Flame of that supernal Light that glowed upon Sinai,"* the *"Remembrance of God"* concerning Whom *"a separate Covenant hath been established with each and every Prophet"* had, through His advent, at once fulfilled the promise of all ages and ushered in the consummation of all Revelations. He the "Qá'im" (He Who ariseth) promised to the Shí'ahs, the "Mihdí" (One Who is guided) awaited by the Sunnís, the "Return of John the Baptist" expected by the Christians, the "Ushídar-Máh" referred to in the Zoroastrian scriptures, the "Return of Elijah" anticipated by the Jews, Whose Revelation was to show forth *"the signs and tokens of all the Prophets,"* Who was to *"manifest the perfection of Moses, the radiance of Jesus and the patience of Job"* had appeared, proclaimed His Cause, been mercilessly persecuted and died gloriously. The *"Second Woe,"* spoken of in the Apocalypse of St. John the Divine, had, at long last, appeared, and the first of the two *"Messengers,"* Whose appearance had been prophesied in the Qur'an, had been sent down.[13]

* Bahá'u'lláh
** Bahá'u'lláh

Shoghi Effendi connected several comments from Daniel with the Dispensation of the Báb. (See Chapter 8)

The *"cleansing of the Sanctuary,"* prophesied by Daniel and confirmed by Jesus Christ in His reference to *"the abomination of desolation,"* had been accomplished. The *"day whose length shall be a thousand years,"* foretold by the Apostle of God [Muhammed] in His Book, had terminated. The *"forty and two months,"* [1,260 years] during which the *"Holy City,"* as predicted by St. John the Divine, would be trodden under foot, had elapsed. The *"time of the end"* had been ushered in.[14]

The response to this release of divine energy was swift and twofold. A wide cross-section of all segments of society, from learned *ulamas*[15] to the illiterate poor, embraced the Message of the Báb. At the same time, the royal authorities and the fanatical Islamic clergy spurred a merciless persecution of the new Bábí community. The Báb was imprisoned about half of His ministry while His followers risked their lives teaching His Faith throughout Persia. During these years of imprisonment in severe conditions, He revealed many works called epistles, or tablets, that fearlessly proclaimed His identity, mission, and teachings.

At one point, the Báb's jailers took Him from his cell in the forbidding mountain fortress at Chihriq to the nearby city of Tabriz in northern Persia. There waited the crown prince, various dignitaries of the Shah, and Islamic clergy trembling at the speed with which the Bábí movement had spread. At the rate it was progressing, it would threaten Islamic institutions and the clergy. Therefore, these leaders decided to invite the Báb to meet with them so that they could entice Him to forsake His mission. The ensuing encounter was reported by a witness:

The majesty of His gait, the expression of overpowering confidence which sat upon His brow—above all, the spirit of power which shone from His whole being, appeared to have for a moment crushed the soul out of the body of those whom He had greeted. A deep, a mysterious silence, suddenly fell upon them. Not one soul in that distinguished assembly dared breathe a single word. At last the stillness which brooded over them was broken by the Nizámu'l-'Ulamá' [a high official of the Shah's court]. "Whom do you claim to be," he asked the Báb, "and what is the message which you have brought?" *"I am,"* thrice exclaimed the Báb, *"I am, I am, the Promised One! I am the One whose name you have for a thousand years invoked, at whose mention you have risen, whose advent you have longed to witness, and the hour of whose Revelation you have prayed God to hasten. Verily I say, it is incumbent upon the peoples of both the East and the West to obey My word and to pledge allegiance to My person."*[16]

The assembled dignitaries could not countenance the Báb's proclamation. Within a day or two, they subjected Him to the bastinado, restraining Him with His bare feet in stocks and repeatedly caning His soles. The purpose of the bastinado was not only to draw blood and cause immense pain, but also to flay the skin off the soles by causing such bruising that the skin of the soles burst. In that condition, they returned Him to His cell in Chiriq.

Finally, on July 9, 1850, in the main square in Tabriz, a firing squad publicly executed the Báb. For many years, His followers protected His remains, hiding them from His enemies until they could be transported to Haifa in Ottoman Palestine. In 1909, His earthly remains were entombed on Mount Carmel. The Shrine of the Báb, which is the second most holy place for Baha'is,[17] is located on the grounds of the Baha'i World Centre, which is also home to the global administrative center of the Baha'i Faith. The nineteen terraced gardens on Mount Carmel, completed in the late twentieth century, include one upon which the Shrine of the Báb stands, with nine above and nine more below.

The Báb had come to one of the most morally degenerate societies in the world. His announcement that humanity stood at the threshold of a new era of spiritual and moral reformation aroused excitement and hope. The message spread like wildfire through the downtrodden population. But the response of the Shah, his royal authorities, and the Islamic clergy was swift and merciless. About twenty thousand Bábís were massacred as, later, were many thousands of Baha'is. Most of the Báb's disciples and the foremost teachers of His Faith lost their lives in the turmoil and pogroms fomented by their enemies.

The nine-year Dispensation of the Báb was the shortest divine Dispensation in the history of revealed religions because one of its two major purposes was to foretell the appearance of *"Him Whom God will make manifest."* His Dispensation started in May 1844 and lasted until late 1852, when Bahá'u'lláh received a message from the Holy Spirit of His identity.

The Báb was the return of the spirit of Elijah—a fascinating story. *"As they [Elijah and Elisha] were walking along and talking together, suddenly a chariot of fire and horses of fire appeared and separated the two of them, and Elijah went up to heaven in a whirlwind."* (2

Kings 2:11) Malachi, the last of the canonical prophets in the Hebrew Bible, foretold that Elijah would come again: *"See, I will send the prophet Elijah to you before that great and dreadful day of the Lord comes."* (Malachi 4:5)

The Jews expected Elijah to literally, physically descend from heaven before the coming of the Messiah. One reason they did not recognize Jesus as the Messiah was because they did not see a literal return of Elijah. In addition, both John the Baptist and Jesus denied that they were Elijah. The apparent nonappearance of Elijah confused Jesus's disciples, especially Peter, James, and John, who witnessed the Transfiguration— the appearance of Moses and Elijah with Jesus. While walking down the mountain afterward, they asked Jesus why the teachers of the law said that Elijah must come first. Jesus replied:

> *To be sure, Elijah comes and will restore all things. But I tell you, Elijah has already come, and they did not recognize him, but have done to him everything they wished. In the same way the Son of Man is going to suffer at their hands. Then the disciples understood that he was talking to them about John the Baptist.* (Matthew 17:10–13)

More than nineteen centuries later, 'Abdu'l-Bahá explained that the return of Elijah referred not to the return of his body but to that of his spiritual attributes:

> *The reason is that we consider here not the individuality of the person but the reality of his perfections—that is to say, the very same perfections that Elias possessed were realized in John the Baptist as well. Thus, John the Baptist was*

*the promised Elias. What is being considered here
is not the essence* but the attributes.*[18]

* That is, the individuality of John.

Shoghi Effendi spoke of the Báb as the return of Elijah
when he made the following comments about the deeply
significant occasion of the interment of the Báb's mortal
remains on Mount Carmel in 1909:

> *With the transference of the remains of the Báb—
> Whose advent marks the return of the Prophet
> Elijah—to Mt. Carmel, and their interment in
> that holy mountain, not far from the cave of that
> Prophet Himself, the Plan so gloriously envisaged
> by Bahá'u'lláh, in the evening of His life, had been
> at last executed, and the arduous labors associated
> with the early and tumultuous years of the ministry
> of the appointed Center of His Covenant ['Abdu'l-
> Bahá] crowned with immortal success.*[19]

Elijah was closely associated with Mount Carmel
because he lived in one or more of the caves on the
mountain's northwest slope in present-day Haifa, Israel.
Tradition holds that Elijah meditated on Mount Carmel
before his encounter with the prophets of Baal and
that he started a school of prophets on the mountain.
Today there are two caves in Haifa associated with
Elijah. One is at the foot of the mountain and is used for
Jewish prayer. The other is a short distance higher on
the mountain under the Stella Maris Church, next to the
Stella Maris monastery, which is the world headquarters
of the Carmelite order of monks. Both caves are within
walking distance of the Shrine of the Báb but the Stella
Maris cave is closest.

This clarification of the meaning of the "return" of Elijah applies to the return of all Prophets of God. Bahá'u'lláh wrote that Jesus tried to explain this concept to His disciples:

> Thus it is that Jesus, Himself, declared: "I go away and come again unto you." [John 14:28] Consider the sun. Were it to say now, "I am the sun of yesterday," it would speak the truth. And should it, bearing the sequence of time in mind, claim to be other than that sun, it still would speak the truth. In like manner, if it be said that all the days are but one and the same, it is correct and true. And if it be said, with respect to their particular names and designations, that they differ, that again is true. For though they are the same, yet one doth recognize in each a separate designation, a specific attribute, a particular character. Conceive accordingly the distinction, variation, and unity characteristic of the various Manifestations of holiness, that thou mayest comprehend the allusions made by the creator of all names and attributes to the mysteries of distinction and unity, and discover the answer to thy question as to why that everlasting Beauty should have, at sundry times, called Himself by different names and titles.[20]

Bahá'u'lláh wrote at length about the united mission of the Prophets and their stations, the first of which is the station of unity:

> It is clear and evident to thee that all the Prophets are the Temples of the Cause of God, Who have appeared clothed in divers attire. If thou wilt observe with discriminating eyes, thou wilt behold

them all abiding in the same tabernacle, soaring in the same heaven, seated upon the same throne, uttering the same speech, and proclaiming the same Faith. Such is the unity of those Essences of being, those Luminaries of infinite and immeasurable splendour.[21]

The second station of each prophet is that of distinction:

The other is the station of distinction, and pertaineth to the world of creation and to the limitations thereof. In this respect, each Manifestation of God hath a distinct individuality, a definitely prescribed mission, a predestined Revelation, and specially designated limitations. Each one of them is known by a different name, is characterized by a special attribute, fulfils a definite Mission, and is entrusted with a particular Revelation.[22]

Not surprisingly, there are many parallels between the earthly missions of the Prophets of God, despite their distinctive stations. This is especially true in the case of Jesus and the Báb. (See Appendix C)

CHAPTER 8

Daniel: 70 Weeks
and 1,260, 1,290, and 1,335 Days

D aniel was an equal opportunity prophet. He
included in his prophecies key dates in Jewish,
Christian, Islamic, Bábí, and Baha'i history. One
vision prophesied the ministry of Jesus and the year of
His crucifixion.

The Seventy Weeks

Daniel was praying to God when he had a vision
about seventy sevens. The angel Gabriel, whom he had
seen in an earlier vision, came to him and said:

> "Seventy 'sevens' are decreed for your people
> and your holy city to finish transgression, to put
> an end to sin, to atone for wickedness, to bring in
> everlasting righteousness, to seal up vision and
> prophecy and to anoint the Most Holy Place.
>
> "Know and understand this: From the time the word
> goes out to restore and rebuild Jerusalem until the
> Anointed One, the ruler, comes, there will be seven
> 'sevens,' and sixty-two 'sevens.' It will be rebuilt
> with streets and a trench, but in times of trouble.
> After the sixty-two 'sevens,' the Anointed One will
> be put to death and will have nothing. The people of

the ruler who will come will destroy the city and the sanctuary. The end will come like a flood: War will continue until the end, and desolations have been decreed. He will confirm a covenant with many for one 'seven.' In the middle of the 'seven' he will put an end to sacrifice and offering. And at the temple he will set up an abomination that causes desolation, until the end that is decreed is poured out on him." (Daniel 9:24–27)

Remember that a day equals a year in biblical timekeeping, so seven days is seven years. Seventy times seven years equals 490 years. The edict of Artaxerxes, which authorized the rebuilding of Jerusalem in 457 BCE, is the starting date for counting the 490 years. Jesus was crucified in the year 33 CE. Adding the number 457 to 33 brings the total to 490 years.

'Abdu'l-Bahá explained a second way to understand the 490 years, or "seventy sevens":

But in Daniel 9:25 this is expressed in another manner, that is, as seven weeks and sixty-two weeks, which outwardly differs from the first statement. How can reference be made to seventy weeks in one place and to sixty-two weeks and seven weeks in another? These two statements do not accord.

In reality, Daniel is referring to two different dates. One begins with the edict Artaxerxes issued to Ezra to rebuild Jerusalem, and corresponds to the seventy weeks which came to an end with the ascension of Christ, when sacrifice and oblation were ended through His martyrdom. The second begins after the completion of the rebuilding of Jerusalem, which is sixty-two weeks until the ascension of Christ. The rebuilding of Jerusalem took seven weeks, which is the equivalent of forty-nine years. Seven weeks added to sixty-two weeks makes sixty-nine weeks, and in the last week the ascension of Christ took place. This completes the seventy weeks, and no contradiction remains.[1]

The 1,260 Years

The twelfth and last chapter of Daniel focuses on the "end times" or the "time of the end." In a vision, Daniel was shown an interesting, possible connection between Michael and Bahá'u'lláh.

> *"At that time Michael, the great prince who protects your people, will arise. There will be a time of distress such as has not happened from the beginning of nations until then. But at that time your people—everyone whose name is found written in the book—will be delivered. Multitudes who sleep in the dust of the earth will awake: some to everlasting life, others to shame and everlasting contempt. Those who are wise will shine like the brightness of the heavens, and those who lead many to righteousness, like the stars for ever and ever. But you, Daniel, roll up and seal the words of the scroll until the time of the end. Many will go here and there to increase knowledge."* (Daniel 12:1–4)

The name Michael means "one like God." In addition to the mention of Michael above in Chapter 12, he is also mentioned in Chapter 10: *"But the prince of the Persian kingdom resisted me twenty-one days. Then Michael, one of the chief princes, came to help me, because I was detained there with the king of Persia."* (Daniel 10:13)

Bahá'u'lláh was born into a Persian noble family that descended from Yazdigird III, the thirty-eighth and last monarch of the Sasanian empire of Persia (224–651 CE). Hence, Bahá'u'lláh was a prince of Persia. His inveterate enemies were the Islamic clergy and the shahs of Persia. Perhaps Michael represents Bahá'u'lláh.

Daniel warned of a time of distress more severe than any since the beginning of nations, marked by suffering more tremendous than any seen before. Of these times Bahá'u'lláh wrote:

> The world is in travail, and its agitation waxeth day by day. Its face is turned towards waywardness and unbelief. Such shall be its plight, that to disclose it now would not be meet and seemly. Its perversity will long continue. And when the appointed hour is come, there shall suddenly appear that which shall cause the limbs of mankind to quake. Then, and only then, will the Divine Standard be unfurled, and the Nightingale of Paradise warble its melody.[2]

The symbolic meaning of the *"multitudes who sleep in the dust of the earth"* is the condition of spiritual unawareness in which many people live, while some individuals shine spiritually and *"lead many to righteousness."* It is unfortunate that adversity that will cause *"the limbs of mankind to quake"* may be required to awaken humanity to Bahá'u'lláh's message.

In his vision, Daniel asked the eternal question "when?" and received an answer in terms of biblical counting. He also received the message to move on with his life because the meanings of his visions were sealed until the end of time:

> Then I, Daniel, looked, and there before me stood two others, one on this bank of the river and one

on the opposite bank. One of them said to the man clothed in linen, who was above the waters of the river, "How long will it be before these astonishing things are fulfilled?"

The man clothed in linen, who was above the waters of the river, lifted his right hand and his left hand toward heaven, and I heard him swear by him who lives forever, saying, "It will be for a time, times and half a time. When the power of the holy people has been finally broken, all these things will be completed."

I heard, but I did not understand. So I asked, "My lord, what will the outcome of all this be?"

He replied, "Go your way, Daniel, because the words are rolled up and sealed until the time of the end. Many will be purified, made spotless and refined, but the wicked will continue to be wicked. None of the wicked will understand, but those who are wise will understand." (Daniel 12:5–10)

"A time, times and half a time" translates to three and a half years. At 360 days each, that equals 1,260 biblical days or calendar years. 'Abdu'l-Bahá commented:

As I have already explained the meaning of "day", no further explanation is needed, but let me briefly say that each day of the Father is equivalent to one year, and each year consists of twelve months. Thus three and a half years makes forty-two months, and forty-two months is 1,260 days, and each day in the Bible is equivalent to one year. And it is in the very year 1260 from the emigration of Muhammad, according to the Muslim calendar, that the Báb, the Herald of Bahá'u'lláh, revealed His mission.[3]

From what date does the counting begin? The emigration refers to the Hegira, the flight of Muhammad and His followers from Mecca to Medina in 622 CE, which was later designated the first year of the Islamic calendar (1 AH). Adding 1,260 *lunar* years to 622 reaches the year 1844—the advent of the Báb. This math only works using the lunar years in the Islamic calendar.

Shia Islam regarded the year 1260 AH, or 1844 CE, as prophetically special because it marked one thousand *lunar* years after the disappearance of the twelfth Imam, which began the period of occultation.

The 1,290 Days

Daniel's last vision also offered the number 1,290 to ponder. *"From the time that the daily sacrifice is abolished and the abomination that causes desolation is set up, there will be 1,290 days."* (Daniel 12:11) There are 1,290 *lunar* years from the date of Muhammad's declaration of His station as a Prophet of God in 613 CE to Bahá'u'lláh's public declaration of His station as a Prophet of God in 1863 CE. 'Abdu'l-Bahá explained:

> *The commencement of this lunar reckoning is from the day of the proclamation of the prophethood of Muhammad in the land of Hijáz; and that was three years after the revelation of His mission, because in the beginning the prophethood of Muhammad was concealed, and no one knew of it save Khadíjih and Ibn-i-Nawfal,* until it was publicly announced three years later. And it was in the year 1290 from the proclamation of the mission of Muhammad that Bahá'u'lláh announced His Revelation.* ** 4*

* That is, Muhammad's wife and her cousin Varaqih-Ibn-i-Nawfal.
** As Muhammad began His public ministry ten years before the Hijrah, this date corresponds to A.H. 1280, or A.D. 1863.

The 1,335 Years

Reverting to solar years, Daniel gives his final numerical prophecy and is then told that his mission on earth is finished.

> *"Blessed is the one who waits for and reaches the end of the 1,335 days.*
>
> *"As for you, go your way till the end. You will rest, and then at the end of the days you will rise to receive your allotted inheritance."* (Daniel 12:12–13)

The 1,335 solar years start with the year 628 CE, the year Muhammad signed a treaty with His enemies in Mecca that signified the Muslim community's recognition as a legitimate force in Medina. This agreement gave Muslims the freedom to move unmolested throughout Arabia.

The 1,335 solar years added to 628 equals 1,963, or the year 1963 CE, which was momentous in Baha'i history. That was the year when members of the fifty-six National Spiritual Assemblies established at that point cast secret ballots to elect the nine-member Universal House of Justice—the global administrative body of the Baha'i Faith—for the first time.

'Abdu'l-Bahá elaborated on the meaning of the 1,335 years for Baha'is in a tablet he wrote to a Kurdish friend:

> *Now concerning the verse in Daniel, the interpretation whereof thou didst ask, namely, "Blessed is he who cometh unto the thousand three hundred and thirty-five days." These days must be reckoned as solar and not lunar years. For according to this calculation a century will have elapsed from the dawn of the Sun of Truth, then will the teachings*

of God be firmly established upon the earth, and the Divine Light shall flood the world from the East even unto the West. Then, on this day, will the faithful rejoice.[5]

The year 1963 concluded the Ten Year Plan (1953-1963), also called the Ten Year Crusade, that Shoghi Effendi launched to facilitate an organized expansion of the Faith. He wrote, *"We are embarked upon the greatest spiritual drama the world has ever witnessed; ..."*[6]

CHAPTER 9

Muhammad, the Seal of the Prophets

It is written in the Qur'an that Muhammad said He was the Seal of the Prophets: *"Muhammad is not the father of any of your men, but (he is) the Messenger of Allah, and the Seal of the Prophets, and Allah has full knowledge of all things."* (Qur'an 33:40, Yusuf Ali translation) Traditional beliefs hold that this verse meant no other Prophets of God would come after Muhammad, despite the prophecies and hadiths referring to the Mahdi, or the Qa'im, as previously explained. But two more Prophets did come in the nineteenth century, the Báb and Bahá'u'lláh. The concepts of *progressive revelation* and *cycles of religion* offer a different understanding of this Qur'anic verse, one that is not at odds with a Revelation following that of Muhammad.

The Baha'i writings explain that God has sent—and will continue to send—a series of Prophets, all of whom confirm the eternal truths, the spiritual teachings of previous Prophets. In addition, when the level of a people's understanding has evolved, a Prophet imparts higher levels of spiritual understanding than previous Prophets were able to do. An analogy for progressive revelation can be made that compares levels of spiritual growth with the education of children in school. Children must learn the basics first and more advanced concepts later. They must be taught the alphabet before they can learn to read and simple mathematics must precede algebra and calculus. Jesus lamented, *"I have much more to say to you, more than you can now bear."* (John 16:12) However, He did speak of the day when the next Prophet would come:

> *But when he, the Spirit of truth, comes, he will guide you into all the truth. He will not speak on his own; he will speak only what he hears, and he will tell you what is yet to come. He will glorify me because it is from me that he will receive what he will make known to you. All that belongs to the Father is mine. That is why I said the Spirit will receive from me what he will make known to you.* (John 16:13–15)

Each of the divinely sent Prophets also cancelled some of the previous divinely ordained social laws and introduced new ones appropriate for the time. For example, Jesus nullified the Jewish laws of divorce and the Sabbath. These changes inspired the early church to drop many Jewish laws that were no longer relevant to the spirit of Christ and the early Christian community.

Thus have the Prophets of God functioned within the system sometimes called progressive revelation. And so has mankind received its spiritual education incrementally in accordance with its capacity.

The Baha'i writings allude to many Prophets, now mostly remembered only in legends and myths, whom God sent at various times to countless peoples on earth. Divine light has shone everywhere among humanity at one time or another. The most famous of these great souls, the ones remembered most vividly today as founders of still-existent world religions, are Abraham, Moses,

Zoroaster, Buddha, Krishna, Jesus, and Muhammad. Then came the Báb and Bahá'u'lláh.

Bahá'u'lláh described these Prophets as pure reflections of God, as mirrors reflecting God's beauty, might, and glory while taking human form. He wrote, *"These Mirrors will everlastingly succeed each other, and will continue to reflect the light of the Ancient of Days."*[1]

Each Prophet of God brought a divinely-revealed message for the spiritual progress of humanity: *"He hath manifested unto man the Day Stars of His divine guidance, the Symbols of His divine unity, and hath ordained the knowledge of these sanctified Beings to be identical with the knowledge of His own self."*[2] The Prophets had a twofold mandate. First, they were to liberate men from the darkness of ignorance and guide them to spiritual light. Second, building on the first, they were to ensure the peace and tranquility of mankind and to provide the means by which that could be established. Bahá'u'lláh wrote about the chain of Revelations that linked the Prophets:

> *Contemplate with thine inward eye the chain of successive Revelations that hath linked the Manifestation of Adam with that of the Báb. I testify before God that each one of these Manifestations hath been sent down through the operation of the Divine Will and Purpose, that each hath been the bearer of a specific Message, that each hath been entrusted with a divinely-revealed Book and been commissioned to unravel the mysteries of a mighty Tablet. The measure of the Revelation with which every one of them hath been identified had been definitely fore-ordained.*[3]

Many of the teachings of the earlier Prophets have been lost, although a few memories were preserved through allegorical mythology. This is how the symbolic accounts of Adam and Noah survived, as well as aspects of other Revelations from preliterate times. Although the scribes who later committed this divine heritage to writing may not have understood the inner meanings, they were somehow compelled to protect these records and to ultimately include them in the canon of the Hebrew Bible.

The Adamic Cycle of progressive revelation—also called the Prophetic Cycle or the Prophetic Era—unfolded throughout the world over about six thousand years. The succession of Prophets of God in this cycle, each with His own Revelation and Book, whether written or given verbally to preliterate peoples, culminated with the advent of Muhammad. The Báb, as the fulfillment of Jewish, Christian, and Islamic prophecies, closed the Adamic Cycle. The Baha'i Cycle, also called the Cycle of Fulfillment, started with the missions of the Báb and Bahá'u'lláh, whose teachings—and those of Bahá'u'lláh's successors yet to come—will ultimately bring humankind to spiritual maturity. The coming of the Báb in 1844 linked the Adamic cycle to the Cycle of Fulfillment. Together, they constitute a universal cycle. 'Abdu'l-Bahá explained:

> Each of the Manifestations [Prophets] of God has likewise a cycle wherein His religion and His law are in full force and effect. When His cycle is ended through the advent of a new Manifestation, a new cycle begins. Thus, cycles are inaugurated, concluded, and renewed, until a universal cycle is completed in the world of existence and momentous

events transpire which efface every record and trace of the past; then a new universal cycle begins in the world, for the realm of existence has no beginning. ... We are in the cycle which began with Adam and whose universal Manifestation is Bahá'u'lláh.[4]

In that context, Muhammad was the last Prophet in the Adamic Cycle, which was closed by the Báb. Muhammad was the Seal of the Prophets for the Adamic Cycle.

Each Prophet has also foretold the coming of the next. The related prophecies have often been misunderstood by followers to mean a literal return of their Prophet or of someone connected with Him. However, these prophecies of a return meant the reemergence of the spiritual characteristics of the Prophets in a new Holy Being, who brings new teachings and social laws appropriate for continuing education.

These Holy Beings occupy special stations far beyond those of humans. Their missions have indeed been to save us from sin and to educate us so that we can we can grow spiritually and claim our divine heritage. Bahá'u'lláh explained that humanity's true nature and destiny are beyond human comprehension:

Man is the supreme Talisman. Lack of a proper education hath, however, deprived him of that which he doth inherently possess. Through a word proceeding out of the mouth of God he was called into being; by one word more he was guided to recognize the Source of his education; by yet another word his station and destiny were safeguarded. The Great Being saith: Regard man as a mine rich in gems of inestimable value.[5]

Religion is of primary importance to spiritual education as Bahá'u'lláh explained:

> As the body of man needeth a garment to clothe it, so the body of mankind must needs be adorned with the mantle of justice and wisdom. Its robe is the Revelation vouchsafed unto it by God. Whenever this robe hath fulfilled its purpose, the Almighty will assuredly renew it. For every age requireth a fresh measure of the light of God. Every Divine Revelation hath been sent down in a manner that befitted the circumstances of the age in which it hath appeared.[6]

The decline of religion has created a hole that people try in vain to fill with rampant consumerism, chemical addictions, a deplorable decline in standards of morality, veneration of celebrities, and other evils, not understanding that the true purpose of religion is to be "a radiant light and an impregnable stronghold for the protection and welfare of the peoples of the world, for the fear of God impelleth man to hold fast to that which is good, and shun all evil. Should the lamp of religion be obscured, chaos and confusion will ensue, and the lights of fairness, of justice, of tranquillity and peace cease to shine."[7]

CHAPTER 10

The Divine Springtime

The new spiritual energy triggered by the coming of a Prophet of God manifests not only in the spiritual advancement of a people but also in a rapid development of civilization in the arts and sciences, medicine and architecture, literature and mathematics, and other areas. Historians are familiar with these bursts of creativity, artistry, and inventiveness, but they have not connected them to the infusion of divine revelation into the world. However, the repeated convergence of these two factors is evident after reflection.

Fascinating is the possibility of a cause-and-effect connection between the Prophet Adam and the sudden development of city-states in Sumeria, which historians call the cradle of civilization. There is no surviving written evidence for Adam from the time of His Revelation, although faint memories of His legacy are recorded in Genesis 2:4–25 through 3:1–24. This mythology from the distant past undoubtedly has symbolic meanings that are important for humanity today, but an exploration of that topic is beyond the scope of this book, as is a discussion of references to Adam in the Qur'an. However, the mysterious rise of city-states and the burgeoning technology in Sumeria seems to set the example for more recent instances of divine springtimes.

The Irish Bishop James Ussher (1581–1656) searched for the date of the Creation by studying the timeline of biblical events using a literal reading of the Hebrew Bible. He paid particular attention to the genealogy of "begats" and the historical time references given for the monarchies and postexilic periods up to the time of Christ. His conclusion was that the world was created and Adam was expelled from the Garden of Eden in 4004 BCE. Ussher's chronological calculations were broadly accepted for two centuries until early geologists and other scientists learned that the earth was billions of years old and that life on it could be traced back for millions of years.

While Ussher's calculations were incorrect for the beginning of the world, they might have inadvertently pinpointed the approximate time of the Prophet Adam. Is it only a coincidence that Sumerian civilization developed rapidly in the fourth millennium BCE? Perhaps not. Adam, like every succeeding Prophet of God, released spiritual energy into the world, thus triggering a divine springtime. Nothing remains of Adam's teachings except mythic memories and symbolism. But the flowering of Sumeria has been well explored and documented by archeologists and historians.

The first city-states identified by historians were in Sumeria and they contained monumental temple compounds, palaces, and markets. Extensive irrigation projects expanded agricultural economies. Yokes and harnesses were invented to hitch animals to carts and plows, which plunged four times deeper into the soil than the hoe used by Neolithic farmers. Pastoral advances included the introduction of milk, yogurt, and cheese into the diet and the use of wool in textile creation. Sumerians invented the sailboat and the potter's wheel. Their donkey-drawn carts and horse-drawn chariots revolutionized trade and warfare, respectively. Cuneiform, or wedge writing, emerged as the world's first known system of writing; it may have been invented for commercial use as early as 3800 BCE. Accounting systems evolved to accommodate commercial and centralized administrative needs.

The Sumerians developed a mathematical system based on the number 60 that is still used globally today for hours, minutes, and seconds. This original sexagesimal system enabled the Sumerians to calculate roots, multiply into millions, and use fractions. Mathematics still counts 360 degrees in a circle and 12 inches in a foot. These people looked to the skies and developed astronomy, the lunar calendar, and the sun dial. The science of architecture advanced rapidly as the pulley, lever, saw, chisel, brick mold, arch, vault, and dome opened new possibilities in engineering and construction. The Sumerians built monumental stone sculptures and stepped temples decorated with engraving and inlay work.

It appears that Sumeria experienced a divine springtime and high summer, as evidenced by the rapid advancements of its civilization. Possibly the springtime of Adam's Dispensation kick-started civilization as we know it today. Although no trace of Adam's teachings survived to our day, He would undoubtedly have taught the spiritual verities at a level that could be understood by the people of that time. The degeneration of these teachings may have been evidenced in the emergence of an elaborate pantheon of an uncountable number of deities that appeared along with the belief that humanity had been created to serve them. Perhaps this is evidence that Sumeria eventually experienced the spiritual seasons of autumn and winter of the Adamic Revelation.

The Prophet Abraham, who was probably born in Sumeria, grew up in a polytheistic culture during the winter of Adam's revelation. The book of Genesis devotes more than fourteen chapters (11:26 to 25:10) to Abraham. The Qur'an also recounts Abraham's story at length, starting with his youth in Sumeria where, as the son of an idol maker, he defied the idol cults and confronted the ruler Nimrod about the falsity of idolatry. Nimrod banished Abraham from his homeland, so He relocated to the land of Canaan and taught the singularity of God to another idol-worshipping people. Abraham was followed by Moses, who brought an extensive code of religious law. The Israelite culture subsequently flowered with nation-building energy and a growing level of adult male literacy accompanied by a reverence for written scripture.

The spiritual energy of early Christianity gave rise to Byzantine culture. Generally, the start of the Byzantine Empire is seen as 330 CE, when Constantine I declared a new Rome on the site of the Greek colony of Byzantium. When Constantine converted to Christianity, he brought his empire into the new faith and dedicated a "New Rome" on the site of ancient Byzantium, today's Istanbul, located strategically on the Straight of Bosporus connecting the Sea of Marmara and the Aegean to the Black Sea, and separating the continents of Europe and Asia. While the western half of the Roman Empire fell in the fifth century, its eastern half grew and flourished as the Byzantine Empire. Lasting about a thousand years, it was known for its advances in religious art that influenced Italian Renaissance art. Byzantium became the center for the

Eastern Orthodox Church and for learning and the arts. Ruins of Byzantine churches and their exquisite tile floors can be found throughout the Middle East.

Islamic culture, whose golden age spanned from the eighth to the thirteenth centuries CE—a time known as the medieval era in the western Christian world—emerged from the barbarism of Arabian tribes who constantly raided each other and often buried their female infants alive. A learned, Islamic culture burgeoned with tremendous advances in science, mathematics, medicine, architecture, education, art, and literature. The multicultural Islamic city of Cordoba in today's Spain boasted indoor plumbing, paved streets with miles of public lighting, fountains and gardens, bookstores on every block, and a dynamic economy based on robust trade with partners as far away as China. The library of al-Hakam II (caliph from 961 to 976 CE) is reputed to have held four hundred thousand volumes.

The Bábí and Baha'i Revelations are closely connected with the emergence of major social and technological revolutions of modern times—especially the communications revolution. For example, on May 24, 1844, one day after the Báb revealed His identity to Mulla Husayn in Shiraz, Samuel Morse sent his first telegraph message, *"What hath God wrought?"* (Numbers 23:23, KJV) from Washington, D.C., to Baltimore, reinvigorating a communications revolution that had seen little progress since the invention of the printing press six hundred years before, and triggering the development of electronics technology to the point where information can be sent globally within seconds. The immensity of the outpouring of spiritual energy by the twin Prophets, the Báb and Bahá'u'lláh, is reflected in civilizational advancements that may seem normal to us but whose scope and speed are unprecedented in human history. For example, in the United States, 458 patents were issued in 1840[1] and that number increased steadily year-by-year to 318,849 in 2017.[2]

With His Revelation, Bahá'u'lláh renewed springtime for the whole world, not just a particular ethnic or religious group. He did not abrogate previous religions but endeavored to help their followers obtain a better understanding of their Messengers and scriptures, all of which taught basic spiritual verities and foretold the coming of a future Prophet. Like all previous Prophets whom He not only recognized but honored, Bahá'u'lláh reinforced the spiritual truths taught from time immemorial. He also brought new spiritual teachings designed to help humanity transition from its adolescence to full maturity.

The fragrances of His divine springtime continue wafting on the breezes today. Unfortunately, there is always resistance to a new Revelation. The social problems of today are a symptom of this resistance to the true nature of God and His Revelations. Bahá'u'lláh explained:

> The vitality of men's belief in God is dying out in every land; nothing short of His wholesome medicine can ever restore it. The corrosion of ungodliness is eating into the vitals of human society; what else but the Elixir of His potent Revelation can cleanse and revive it? Is it within human power, O Hakím, to effect in the constituent elements of any of the minute and indivisible particles of matter so complete a transformation as to transmute it into purest gold? Perplexing and difficult as this may

appear, the still greater task of converting satanic strength into heavenly power is one that We have been empowered to accomplish. The Force capable of such a transformation transcendeth the potency of the Elixir itself. The Word of God, alone, can claim the distinction of being endowed with the capacity required for so great and far-reaching a change.[3]

The forces of power, corruption, ignorance, and superstition deny the warmth and light of divine truths. However, the sun of the Revelation of Bahá'u'lláh has only recently broken over the horizon. Its rays are strengthening and will continue to do so in the days, years, and centuries ahead.

However, our Millerite friends in the West had no access to any source of knowledge that would explain the divine seasons to them. A literal interpretation of the Gospels gave Adventists no reason to expect the coming of a new Prophet of God. Therefore, they worked with what they had and forged ahead as best they could.

CHAPTER 11

The Sectarian Survivors of Millerism

hristianity was not exempt from the four seasons of a divinely inspired Dispensation. The faith of Jesus flowered in a brutal Roman world and gained converts with its simple teachings that God—the one God who created humankind—was love, and that life in Christ offered eternal life. Its spring and summer would bring profound changes in spiritual consciousness at first to the Middle East and then to the West and eventually to converts throughout the world. However, the fall and winter of Christianity has long been evidenced by religious wars and theological schisms. The Center for the Study of Global Christianity gives the eyebrow-raising number of forty-seven thousand Christian denominations as of 2017.[1]

After the Great Disappointment, the Adventist movement fell to schismatic influences and split into three main groups—the Spiritualizers, the Albany Adventists, and the Sabbatarians. The Spiritualizers turned away from literal biblical interpretation. Instead, they gave spiritualized, or symbolic, meanings to biblical verses, thus making it possible to believe that the Second Coming had occurred in their hearts. The Spiritualizers formed no permanent organizations, though, and its adherents eventually drifted away.

The Albany Adventists continued with literal biblical interpretations concerning the Second Coming. At first they half-heartedly put forth new dates for the event but then gave up on that possibility. The group splintered, with four main organizations emerging—the American Evangelical Conference, established in 1858; the Church of God (Oregon, Illinois), sometime in the 1850s; the Advent Christian Church, in 1860; and the Life and Advent Union, in 1863. Of these four, only the Advent Christian Church survives today. The others declined and died primarily because their theologies differed little from those of evangelical churches, which toward the end of the nineteenth century put more emphasis on the Second Coming and adopted premillennialism.

The Advent Christian Church

The Advent Christian Church was a first-day (Sunday worship) church that initially prospered despite losses to breakaway groups. Advent Christians put doctrinal emphasis on the anticipated Second Coming of Christ and the Last Judgment—and revived the doctrines of *conditionalism* and *annihilationism*, which both Miller and Himes had spoken against and mainstream Adventism did not adopt, although Himes later accepted these doctrines when he joined the Advent Christian Church in 1863. The doctrine of conditionalism states that at physical death the soul enters a state of unconsciousness called soul slumber until the bodily resurrection at the Second Coming, when the person will gain physical immortality only if he or she believed in Christ. David Burge, an Advent Christian in New Zealand, explained:

> The Bible teaches that we do not go to heaven or hell at death. Immortality is something we must

seek after and only the righteous will be given immortality by Jesus Christ at His Coming. Since it is only by faith in Jesus Christ that people are granted immortality we may say that God has made immortality conditional upon faith in Christ. We go to our graves as dead as dead can be. We can only go on living beyond the grave if we are given our lives back again.[2]

The doctrine of annihilationism holds that the souls of the wicked do not go to hell for punishment but are utterly destroyed, or annihilated, for all eternity. Burge explained:

A living soul is not an immortal one. At death the body returns to dust and the spirit, or the breath of life, returns to God who gave it. Without the breath of life the whole person is dead. Hell is not a cosmic torture chamber. It is a Divine garbage dump. It is an incinerator in which all that is sinful or imperfect about this world—all who are in rebellion against God—will be finally destroyed when this world is made new.[3]

(See Appendix D for the full article.)

Aside from conditionalism and annihilationism, Advent Christian theology is similar to that of evangelical Protestantism. However, in the early years, these two doctrines provided the main identity of the Advent Christian Church and were a point of attraction that helped ensure the denomination's survival.

The 1890 United States census showed the membership of the Advent Christian Church as 25,816.[4] In 1925, membership numbered 28,297 and in 2007, the last year for which data was reported, it numbered 23,629.[5] This church has been slowly declining.

The Church of God (Seventh Day)

Sabbatarian Adventists believed that worship must be held on the seventh day, or Saturday. Two Sabbatarian churches have lasted. The Church of God (Seventh Day) was formed in the early 1860s by Sabbatarians who rejected the visions of Ellen White of the Seventh-day Adventist movement, the other Sabbatarian church that has survived. Through the years, the Church of God (Seventh Day) suffered several schisms and reunifications. In 2010, its North American membership numbered fourteen thousand in more than two hundred congregations.[6]

The Seventh-day Adventist Church

The Seventh-day Adventist Church has by far been the most successful church to emerge from Millerism. Early Seventh-day Adventists adopted the doctrines of conditionalism and annihilationism and added the *second sanctuary of heaven*, the *investigative judgment*, and a unique approach to the *open door/shut door* controversy.

The second sanctuary was a new interpretation of Daniel 8:14: *"Unto two thousand and three hundred days; then shall the sanctuary be cleansed."* The cleansing of the sanctuary was previously thought to represent the cleansing of the earth from sin. Because the literal interpretation of the Second Coming and purification of the earth had not come to pass, Adventists provided a new interpretation. Some Millerites still strongly believed that something had indeed happened on October 22, but what?

Late in October 1844, a man named Hiram Edson, a Methodist farmer in Port Gibson, New York, who believed that the faithful would receive guidance and an explanation for the disappointment, had a vision while he was walking through a field with a friend:

> I was stopped about midway and heaven seemed to open to my view.... I saw distinctly, and clearly, that instead of our High Priest coming out of the Most Holy of the heavenly sanctuary to come to this earth on the tenth day of the seventh month, at the end of the 2300 days, that he for the first time entered on that day the second apartment of that sanctuary; and that he had a work to perform in the Most Holy before coming to this earth.[7]

Within the space of a few weeks, a young Millerite woman named Ellen G. Harmon (later Ellen White, 1827–1915) was praying for guidance when she also had a vision that she believed confirmed something had indeed happened. She had been born in Gorham, Maine, and at age nine she was severely injured by a rock thrown at her head by a school mate. She spent three weeks in a coma, never returned to school, and was in poor health for years. The impact undoubtedly caused a traumatic brain injury. Neurologists might ponder the possible connection between that trauma and the visions she later reported having while in a trance state.

The Harmon family moved to Portland, Maine, sometime later and became caught up in the whirlwind of Millerism and Adventism. The Great Disappointment of 1844 did not leave Ellen disheartened as it had so many others. After her local Methodist Church ejected the family for their Millerite beliefs, Ellen's convictions only deepened. One day in December 1844, Ellen fell into a trance and had a vision of the celestial travel of the Advent people to the city of God. She shared this vision and others with fellow Adventists, many of whom accepted them as God's light and guidance.

The essence of Ellen's lengthy vision was that the Advent people were traveling upward along a path illumined from behind with bright light. Their challenge was to keep their attention focused on Jesus, who was leading them to a heavenly city where they would be safe. But many people lost their footing and tumbled into darkness. George R. Knight commented:

> That visionary experience was to change Ellen Harmon's life. Not only did she see herself as having the prophetic gift after that experience, but it also directed her back to the seventh-month movement as a fulfillment of prophecy. From that point to her death in 1915, she saw the October 22 date as a "bright light" to guide God's end-time people. Far from being a mistake or a delusion, the seventh-month movement with its October 22 fulfillment of prophecy became an anchor point in the advent experience. Those who rejected that anchor point, she held, were left in "perfect darkness" and "stumbled and fell." In that sentiment she seemed to be giving what she saw as the fruitless long-term future of the open-door (eventually Albany) Adventists. From her perspective in December 1844, she held that those forms of Adventism that cut loose from their prophetic roots would eventually come to nothing.[8]

A core point of doctrine developed that stated the October event had occurred but in a second sanctuary in heaven—that Jesus went to a second sanctuary and, when His work was finished there, He would return to earth to start His millennial rule. In the meantime, Christ was conducting the investigative judgment from the second sanctuary. The cleansing of the sanctuary was interpreted to mean Christ's judgment of human souls—the determination of who among the living were asleep in Christ and who were abiding in Christ, and who among the dead had been in each category.

The open-door/shut-door controversy also needed resolution. This staple of early Adventist disputes was inspired by Matthew 25:1–13, the parable of the ten virgins who took their lamps and went to meet the bridegroom. Five of the virgins had sufficient oil; the other five did not bring oil and were out trying to buy it when the bridegroom arrived at midnight. The first five were admitted (open-door) to the wedding banquet—the kingdom of heaven, but the door was shut (shut-door) to the other five. Millerism held that the door to salvation would be shut in 1844 with the Second Coming. After Christ did not come, endless arguments erupted about whether the door was open or shut. The Adventists at the Albany conference endorsed the open door, saying that the door to salvation was still open because the Second Advent had not occurred.

Seventh-day Adventists initially held on to the shut-door belief while developing their new doctrine about the cleansing of the sanctuary. However, the shut door became increasingly untenable because it meant that many people would be born and die with no hope of salvation. The resolution to this apparent contradiction took the form of a practical compromise. By the early 1850s, the shut door meant that the door of the Holy Place of the heavenly sanctuary was shut when the first phase of Christ's ministry was completed in 1844; the open door applied to the second phase of His heavenly ministry that began immediately after the end of the first. The door to salvation would be open until the earthly return of Jesus.

Formally established in 1863, the Seventh-day Adventist Church was based on eschatological theology focused on the end times, combined with traditional Christian beliefs in the trinity, baptism, communion, and the Bible as the only sacred text. The Church has always considered itself to be the true heir of Millerism as well as a remnant renewed and called upon to keep the commandments of God and the faith of Jesus.

The completion of the investigative judgment will mark the close of human probation before the Second Advent. When Christ appears, the resurrected righteous and the living righteous will be glorified and caught up to meet their Lord. There will be a thousand-year reign of Christ in heaven, during which time the wicked dead will be judged and the earth will be utterly desolate because it will be occupied by Satan and his angels. After a thousand years, Christ will descend from heaven to earth. The forces of righteousness will defeat Satan and his minions, who will be consumed by the fire of God. The earth will be cleansed and will be free of sin and sinners forever.

Ellen Harmon married James White (1821–1881), one of Miller's earliest and most stalwart supporters. They worked indefatigably as a team to build church congregations, publish tracts and newsletters promoting Adventism, and promote their Adventist beliefs.

Her visions were a major influence on the development of Seventh-day Adventist Church theology. Numbering about two thousand between 1844 and 1909, Ellen White's visions formed the foundation of her testimonies, sermons, and publications. In her writing career, she wrote more than forty books and about five thousand periodical articles on subjects ranging from religion, theology, and her visions, to social relationships, prophecy, publishing, nutrition and health, creationism, and agriculture.

Several of her visions concerned the relationship between physical and spiritual health, especially the importance of a vegetarian diet, exercise, sunshine, clean air, and pure water. The Seventh-day Adventists accepted this emphasis on health reform and to this day the Church encourages a vegetarian diet. It operates many medical facilities and schools throughout the world and strictly prohibits the recreational use of alcohol, tobacco, and narcotics.

White's visions guided the early development of the church in countless ways. Certainty in the validity of White's prophetic ministry is a basic belief of the Seventh-day Adventist Church:

The Scriptures testify that one of the gifts of the Holy Spirit is prophecy. This gift is an identifying mark of the remnant church and we believe it was manifested in the ministry of Ellen G. White. Her writings speak with prophetic authority and provide comfort, guidance, instruction, and correction to the church. They also make clear that the Bible is the standard by which all teaching and experience must be tested.[9]

The Church reported its membership as of 2017 to be a little over 20 million members worldwide, of which 1,356,476 had converted that year, along with the establishment of 2,655 new congregations.[10]

However, the process of obtaining converts to the church has always been easier than keeping them. Church leaders have spent a long time—and counting—since the mid-nineteenth century trying to maintain excitement about the imminent return of Jesus, especially within the context of theology unique to Seventh-day Adventism. In today's increasingly interconnected world, at a time when information on almost any subject is readily available, people show less inclination to embrace exclusionary doctrines. However, even as the Church faces the challenges of materialism, secularism, and the information age, as well as internal issues common to all religious organizations, its achievements are worthy of admiration.

CHAPTER 12

Understanding Matthew 24

As the Millerites and their Adventist descendants learned, the Bible is not as straightforward as readers might wish it to be. Shoghi Effendi wrote, *"Except for what has been explained by Bahá'u'lláh and 'Abdu'l-Bahá, we have no way of knowing what various symbolic allusions in the Bible mean."*[1] Even when the Baha'i writings give meanings for symbols, 'Abdu'l-Bahá urged caution in deciding that any one meaning is intended, saying, *"The Words of God have innumerable significances and mysteries of meanings—each one a thousand and more."*[2] The following exploration keeps these admonitions in mind.

The Gospel of Matthew contains the most extensive account of Jesus speaking about His return in any of the four Gospels. Chapter 24 is devoted to this subject and many people interpret its verses to mean a literal, physical return. However, a symbolic perspective on Matthew 24 offers far more breadth and depth of understanding. It considers the possibility that Jesus spoke within the context of progressive revelation, God's unfailing education for all people throughout all times and ages. *The Kitáb-i-Íqán* (The Book of Certitude),[3] which is regarded as Bahá'u'lláh's preeminent theological work, elaborates extensively on the nature of the Prophets and the successive divine Dispensations offered to humanity. The Baha'i scholar Adib Taherzadeh commented on the *Kitáb-i-Íqán*:

> The great majority of the followers of the world's religions, however, are taught to believe only in one Messenger of God. While sincere in their belief that their religion is true and divine in origin, they often have not recognized the reality of their own Prophet. There is a great deal of difference between having knowledge of a religion and knowing the reality of the Founder of one's Faith.
>
> The *Kitáb-i-Íqán* has enabled a vast number of people from various backgrounds to understand the truth of their own religions, the first step towards believing in Bahá'u'lláh. This book has shed great lustre upon the Holy Books of past Dispensations. It has unfolded the pattern and disclosed the meaning of progressive revelation. It has laid down an enduring foundation for the ultimate unity of all past religions. It has served as a key with which the followers of Bahá'u'lláh have opened doors of knowledge hitherto unknown to man.[4]

Jesus prophesied events that would occur in both the near and far future and He did so in both literal and symbolic terms. For example, one day, Jesus was walking away from the Temple when His disciples approached Him and called His attention to its wonderful buildings. *"Do you see all these things?" Jesus responded, "Truly I tell you, not one stone here will be left on another; every one will be thrown down."* (Matthew 24:2) There could be at least two meanings to this one sentence.

First, Jesus may have been using the Temple as a symbol for His body. After He whipped the merchants out of the Temple courts and told the dove sellers to stop turning His father's house into a market, the Jews asked Him for a sign about where he gained the authority to do such a thing. Jesus responded, *"Destroy this temple, and I will raise it in three days."* (John 2:19) The Jews protested that it had taken forty years to build the Temple. How could Jesus raise it in three days? But the disciples understood that *"the temple he had spoken of was his body."* (John 2:21)

Second, time soon proved that Jesus was also speaking literally of the fate of the Second Temple. In 19 BCE, Herod began the most massive building project of his reign, the rebuilding of the Temple in sumptuous splendor and the doubling in size of the Temple Mount, a stone-paved, rectangular platform on which stood the Temple and various buildings. The massive Antonia fortress occupied the northwest corner with a large reservoir called the Pool of Israel nearby. The complex also included colonnades, a huge hall on the southern end for social and merchant activities, an archives building, and many other structures. The retaining walls enclosing the Temple Mount were fifteen feet thick. This massive construction project took forty-six years to complete. How the Temple must have gleamed in radiant splendor during Jesus's time! Its destruction would have been unthinkable.

Except the unimaginable happened. The Jewish revolt against the Romans began in 66 CE. After four years of war, the Romans defeated the Jews in 70 CE, razed the Temple, and sacked Jerusalem. No stone of the Temple was left standing on another, as Jesus had foreseen.

The twenty-fourth chapter of Matthew then moves on to the Olivet discourse, its name derived from its delivery on the Mount of Olives. *"As Jesus was sitting on the Mount of Olives, the disciples came to him privately. 'Tell us,' they said, 'when will this happen, and what will be the sign of your coming and of the end of the age?'"* (Matthew 24:3) Jesus spoke with His disciples at their level of understanding to describe His return and the events that would surround it. His disciples probably would not have understood or accepted an explanation of progressive revelation or the "return" of a Prophet other than Jesus. Their worldview was too limited for such expansive thinking. Again, Jesus had said: *"I have much more to say to you, more than you can now bear."* (John 16:12) Although He gave some clear statements, He also used symbols and a parable or two to answer their questions. Even though Jesus gently alluded to a new Prophet, the disciples only "heard" that the "return" would be Him. Bahá'u'lláh would later explain the return of a Prophet within the context of the unity of all the Prophets: *"Purge thy sight, therefore, from all earthly limitations, that thou mayest behold them all as the bearers of one Name, the exponents of one Cause, the manifestations of one Self, and the revealers of one Truth, and that thou mayest apprehend the mystic "return" of the Words of God as unfolded by these utterances."*[5]

As explained in Chapter 7, the Prophets of God share the station of unity—they are from one source and teach the same spiritual verities. Each Prophet also has the station of distinction—His own name and individuality, a definitely prescribed mission and Revelation, and specific limitations.

Jesus used clear statements about events that would precede the return—false prophets, wars and rumors of wars, and famines and earthquakes. But people of faith were not to be alarmed: *"All these are the beginning of birth pains."* (Matthew 24:8) There would be religious persecution and martyrdom, an increase of wickedness, and love grown cold, *"but the one who stands firm to the end will be saved."* (Matthew 24:13)

Another answer to the "when?" question was: *"And this gospel of the kingdom will be preached in the whole world as a testimony to all nations, and then the end will come."* (Matthew 24:14) Christian missionary efforts had brought the Hebrew Bible and the New Testament to all parts of the world by the mid-nineteenth century.

Jesus gave another important clue about a definite time for the return: *"So when you see standing in the holy place 'the abomination that causes desolation,' spoken of through the prophet Daniel—let the reader understand."* (Matthew 24:15) Daniel mentioned this abomination three times (Daniel 8:13–14, 9:27, and 12:11–12), the first time with reference to the 2,300 days (solar years ending in 1844 CE), the second to the seventy weeks (ascension of Christ in 33 CE), and the third to the 1,290 days (lunar years ending in 1863 CE). (See Chapter 8)

Jesus warned of the chaos and danger that would ensue: *"Pray that your flight will not take place in winter or on the Sabbath. For then there will be great distress, unequaled from the beginning of the world until now—and never to be equaled again."* (Matthew 24:20–21) However, in neither the United States nor Persia of the 1840s was there such a time of unequaled distress. Perhaps this great distress was not to be experienced until near our time. The global effect of the Dispensation of Bahá'u'lláh has been a measured process. As the rays of the dawn of His Revelation have risen above the horizon, so has a resistance that is magnifying the horrors of wars, the extent of social disintegration, and other areas of great distress. The time and point of the maximum stress between the energy inherent in the Dispensation of Bahá'u'lláh and resistant forces will most likely only be identified in hindsight. Such a massive shift starts slowly and only gradually builds strength and speed. We are now approaching the point where change is discernible from day to day. Even the media with its "breaking news" cycles is having difficulties keeping abreast of changes in human affairs as well as those in the physical world, many caused by global warming and human abuse of the environment.

Fortunately for us, Jesus also foresaw mercy: *"If those days had not been cut short, no one would survive, but for the sake of the elect those days will be shortened."* (Matthew 24:22)

Who are the elect? 'Abdu'l-Bahá told an audience in Paris: *"The great mass of humanity does not exercise real love and fellowship. The elect of humanity are those who live together in love and unity. They are preferable before God because the divine attributes are already manifest in them."*[6] Evidently, the elect are not chosen because of their belief system. They are those individuals who choose to live in harmony with others and to exert efforts that benefit all. 'Abdu'l-Bahá further said: *"It is not through lip-service only that the elect of God have attained to holiness, but by patient lives of active service they have brought light into the world."*[7]

Jesus warned of false prophets for wherever there are carcasses the vultures will gather. He indicated the area of the globe where the return would occur: *"For as lightning that comes from the east is visible even in the west, so will be the coming of the Son of Man."* (Matthew 24:27) Then He referred to Isaiah 13:10 and 34:4 for more clues about the return:

> *Immediately after the distress of those days*
> *'the sun will be darkened,*
> *and the moon will not give its light;*
> *the stars will fall from the sky,*
> *and the heavenly bodies will be shaken.'*
> (Matthew 24:29)

What phenomena would so distress the world? Bahá'u'lláh provided insight:

> *Thus, it hath become evident that the terms "sun," "moon," and "stars" primarily signify the Prophets of God, the saints, and their companions, those Luminaries, the light of Whose knowledge hath shed illumination upon the worlds of the visible and the invisible.*

> *In another sense, by these terms is intended the divines of the former Dispensation, who live in the days of the subsequent Revelations, and who hold the reins of religion in their grasp. If these divines be illumined by the light of the latter Revelation they will be acceptable unto God, and will shine with a light everlasting. Otherwise, they will be declared as darkened, even though to outward seeming they be leaders of men, inasmuch as belief and unbelief, guidance and error, felicity and misery, light and*

darkness, are all dependent upon the sanction of Him Who is the Day-star of Truth.

It is evident and manifest unto every discerning observer that even as the light of the star fadeth before the effulgent splendour of the sun, so doth the luminary of earthly knowledge, of wisdom, and understanding vanish into nothingness when brought face to face with the resplendent glories of the Sun of Truth, the Day-star of divine enlightenment.[8]

In accordance with the spirit of this statement, the darkening of the sun could be the waning of previous Dispensations whose times have passed—whose suns have set. The darkening of the moon could signify the debility of old religious institutions that are no longer able to reflect the rays of the sun of their Prophet. And the falling of the stars could be the decline of those religious leaders who fail to recognize the Prophet for this day and try to judge a new Dispensation by their own standards.

Jesus explained: *"And then shall appear the sign of the Son of man in heaven: and then shall all the tribes of the earth mourn, and they shall see the Son of man coming in the clouds of heaven with power and great glory."* (Matthew 24:30, KJV) Bahá'u'lláh commented on the meanings of this passage:

And now, with reference to His words: "And then shall all the tribes of the earth mourn, and they shall see the Son of man coming in the clouds of heaven with power and great glory." These words signify that in those days men will lament the loss of the Sun of the divine beauty, of the Moon of knowledge, and of the Stars of divine wisdom. Thereupon, they will behold the countenance of the promised One, the adored Beauty, descending from heaven and riding upon the clouds. By this is meant that the divine Beauty will be made manifest from the heaven of the will of God, and will appear in the form of the human temple. The term "heaven" denoteth loftiness and exaltation, inasmuch as it is the seat of the revelation of those Manifestations of Holiness, the Day-springs of ancient glory. These ancient Beings, though delivered from the womb of their mother, have in reality descended from the heaven of the will of God. Though they be dwelling on this earth, yet their true habitations are the retreats of glory in the realms above. They are sent forth through the transcendent power of the Ancient of Days, and are raised up by the exalted will of God, the most mighty King. This is what is meant by the words: "coming in the clouds of heaven."[9]

Bahá'u'lláh further elaborated on the meaning of clouds:

By the term "clouds" is meant those things that are contrary to the ways and desires of men. These "clouds" signify, in one sense, the annulment of laws, the abrogation of former Dispensations, the repeal of rituals and customs current amongst men, the exalting of the illiterate faithful above the learned opposers of the Faith. In another sense, they mean the appearance of that immortal Beauty in the image of mortal man, with such human limitations as eating and drinking, poverty and riches, glory and abasement, sleeping and waking, and such other things as cast doubt in the minds of men, and cause them to turn away. All such veils are symbolically referred to as "clouds." [10]

Only a few people recognize a Prophet with a new Revelation in His time, while most do not see past the "clouds" of entrenched tradition even though the coming is likened to a loud trumpet call: *"And he will send his angels with a loud trumpet call, and they will gather his elect from the four winds, from one end of the heavens to the other."* (Matthew 24:31)

What, or who, are angels? They might be a special creation of God that belongs in its own kingdom and exists to do the will of God. The Kingdom of God is too vast in its spiritual cosmology to reject that possibility. However, angels may be those exalted human souls who are reinforced by the power of the Holy Spirit, who are consumed with the fire of the love of God and have acquired spiritual attributes. 'Abdu'l-Bahá wrote:

> *By angels is meant the divine confirmations and heavenly powers. Angels are also those holy souls who have severed attachment to the earthly world, who are free from the fetters of self and passion and who have attached their hearts to the Divine Realm and the Merciful Kingdom. They are of the Kingdom, heavenly; they are of the Merciful One, divine. They are the manifestations of the divine grace and the dawns of spiritual bounty.* [11]

Jesus gave a graphic description of peoples' response to the coming of a Prophet. *"That is how it will be at the coming of the Son of Man. Two men will be in the field; one will be taken and the other left. Two women will be grinding with a hand mill; one will be taken and the other left."* (Matthew 24:39–41)

The phrase *"to be taken"* has inspired belief in the rapture, the lifting into heaven of the saved. There is much comfort in believing in the literal return of Jesus Christ and His ushering in the Kingdom of God on earth and establishing a thousand years of peace—let *Him* do the work! This kind of escape, though, is not God's plan. This is not why He sends Messenger after Messenger after Messenger. It is humanity's God-given task to grow up, to achieve spiritual maturity. We have been told how to achieve this.

The Baha'i scholar Hushidar Motlagh made a succinct comment: "The rapture is spiritual. It relates to the hearts and souls of humankind. As soon as the awakened ones acknowledge their Lord, they rise to a new realm invisible to others."[12]

Jesus delivered the directive to keep watch and prepare. *"Therefore keep watch, because you do not know on what day your Lord will come,"* (Matthew 24:42) and *"So you also must be ready, because the Son of Man will come at an hour when you do not expect him."* (Matthew 24:44)

Jesus told the parable of the thief in the night to emphasize that the Son of Man would come at an hour and time not expected. He described how the faithful and wise servant fulfilled his duties to his master while the other servant, believing that the master was staying away a long time, abused his fellows and behaved in a wicked manner. Jesus said: *"The master of that servant will come on a day when he does not expect him and at an hour he is not aware of. He will cut him to pieces and assign him a place with the hypocrites, where there will be weeping and gnashing of teeth."* (Matthew 24:50–51)

The Master did not delay his return. God has a divine timetable for sending His Messengers, each of Whom is a return in the station of unity of former ones, each of Whom is a return of the attributes of former ones. However, people usually do not believe that a return has occurred because it was not in accordance with their literal expectations. Or they refuse teachings that do not agree with their traditional beliefs. Motlagh wrote an interesting perspective on this parable of the thief in the night that summarizes the expectation and the reality:

> This prophetic parable implies that many will continue to wait and wish for their Master's return, **after the set time has passed, and after the Master has returned** because they assume that their "master is delaying his coming" (Matthew 24:48, NKJ). The parable of the ten maidens clearly supports this. The five maidens who took no oil, "slumbered and slept" (Matthew 25:5, NKJ) because they thought the Bridegroom would be late. While they were dreaming about his late return, He came and left them absorbed in their dreams.
>
> This prophecy clarifies the point:
>
> *Suddenly, in an instant, the Lord Almighty will come . . . [it will be] as it is with a dream, with a vision in the night—as when a hungry man dreams that he is eating, but he awakens, and his hunger remains; as when a thirsty man dreams that he is drinking, but he awakens faint, with his thirst unquenched.* (Isaiah 29:5–8)
>
> Many people prefer to be dreaming than to be awake, especially if they can choose

their dreams. But as the prophecy declares, dreaming alone or feeling comfortable cannot satisfy the hunger of the spirit.[13]

God is indeed an exact timekeeper. The year 1844, along with other years specified by Daniel, unfolded as convergences in prophecy just as planned.

CHAPTER 13

Bahá'u'lláh, the Glory of God

The prophet Daniel's references to the 1,260 days, the 1,290 days, and the 1,335 days coincided exactly with the declaration of the Báb in 1844, the declaration of Bahá'u'lláh in 1863, and the election of the Universal House of Justice, the pinnacle of the Baha'i Administrative Order, in 1963. Jesus spoke at length in Matthew 24 about the coming of a Prophet of God and the events that would precede that. Shaykh Ahmad and Siyyid Kazim realized that the Qa'im of their search would not lead the people backwards into ninth-century Islam but would bring a new Dispensation. The span of time from Daniel in the sixth century BCE to the early nineteenth century CE is about twenty-five thousand years. Yet Daniel, Jesus, and the Shaykhi movement pointed in varying ways to the coming of the Báb and Bahá'u'lláh, known as the Glory of God.

Bahá'u'lláh was born into a life of immense wealth and leisure. Rather than follow his father into service at the royal court, however, He and His wife devoted themselves to serving the poor. Once He recognized the Báb and entered His service, Bahá'u'lláh and His family saw their fortunes reversed. Bahá'u'lláh was among the few of the Báb's supporters who survived the persecutions of the 1840s and '50s, when it is estimated that twenty thousand were killed. He was tortured and imprisoned in Tehran, Persia, in 1852 and then was sent into forty years of exile and imprisonment.

Bahá'u'lláh suffered severe persecutions the rest of His life, persecutions relentless and unceasing. Before a divine springtime blooms, the last awful days of winter hold on—and Bahá'u'lláh and His family fully experienced them. 'Abdu'l-Bahá wrote:

> There was no persecution, vicissitude or suffering He did not experience at the hand of His enemies and oppressors. All the days of His life were passed in difficulty and tribulation; at one time in prison, another in exile, sometimes in chains. He willingly endured these difficulties for the unity of mankind, praying that the world of humanity might realize the radiance of God, the oneness of humankind become a reality, strife and warfare cease and peace and tranquillity be realized by all. In prison He hoisted the banner of human solidarity, proclaiming Universal Peace, writing to the kings and rulers of nations summoning them to international unity and counselling arbitration. His life was a vortex of persecution and difficulty, yet catastrophes, extreme ordeals and vicissitudes did not hinder the accomplishment of His work and mission.[1]

To the consternation of the authorities and contrary to their expectations, Bahá'u'lláh in exile attracted significant attention as a spiritual leader and teacher. Just days before His departure from Baghdad to further exile, Bahá'u'lláh publicly announced that He was the one foretold by the Báb, *"Him Whom God will make manifest."* His exiles culminated in the prison city of Akka in Ottoman-ruled Palestine did not stop His pen and the torrent of His revelatory outpourings.

Even though authorities along the path of exile usually did not recognize Bahá'u'lláh's station, they were often so affected by His saintly character and gracious demeanor that they improved His conditions of imprisonment. In fact, although Bahá'u'lláh was a prisoner for the entire duration of His forty-year ministry, the authorities in Ottoman Palestine allowed Him to spend the last few years of His life in a large country home in Bahji located a few miles outside Akka and across the bay from Haifa. He lived with a measure of freedom and met with visitors from all walks of life.

Bahá'u'lláh's spirit ascended in 1892. His family and followers put His remains to rest beneath the floor of a garden room in a small house steps from His home at Bahji. Now known as the Shrine of Bahá'u'lláh, this burial location is the most holy place on earth for Baha'is.

Archivists have preserved countless eyewitness accounts of the events surrounding the lives and activities of the Báb and Bahá'u'lláh. Humanity is extraordinarily fortunate that these two Prophets came so relatively recently in history and that the Sacred Texts of the Baha'i Faith are part of modern history. The sheer volume of the writings of the Faith provides the opportunity for a lifetime of study. Bahá'u'lláh described His revelatory writings as an Ocean:

O people! I swear by the one true God! This is the Ocean out of which all seas have proceeded, and with which every one of them will ultimately be united. From Him all the Suns have been generated, and unto Him they will all return. Through His potency the Trees of Divine Revelation have yielded their fruits, every one of which hath been sent down in the form of a Prophet, bearing a Message to God's creatures in each of the worlds whose number God, alone, in His all-encompassing Knowledge, can reckon.[2]

The unification of mankind is a foremost teaching of the Revelation of Bahá'u'lláh. A core tenet of the Baha'i Faith is that God is one, His prophets are one, and humanity is one. World peace will be achieved only when the world's people recognize these three "onenesses." Bahá'u'lláh wrote: *"Ye are all fruits of one tree and the leaves of one branch,*[3] and *"Let not a man glory in that he loves his country; let him rather glory in this, that he loves his kind,"*[4] and *"Let your vision be world-embracing, rather than confined to your own self."*[5] (See Appendix E for a summary of the principles of the Baha'i Faith.)

In addition to unity, the Day of God is a major theme in Bahá'u'lláh's writings. It is the time when a Prophet of God appears and the ensuing time through which His Dispensation is the most recent one. However, a Day of God is not the end of the world and it is not characterized by a sudden removal of human beings from this world to heaven. Instead, it is the time when a new set of divine tools—accompanied by instruction manuals!—are delivered to guide humanity in accomplishing God's work on earth. Bahá'u'lláh elaborated on the many ramifications of the Day of God that accompanies His Dispensation:

This is the Day which the Pen of the Most High hath glorified in all the holy Scriptures. There is no verse in them that doth not declare the glory of His holy

Name, and no Book that doth not testify unto the loftiness of this most exalted theme. Were We to make mention of all that hath been revealed in these heavenly Books and holy Scriptures concerning this Revelation, this Tablet would assume impossible dimensions.[6]

This Day of God has infused God's grace into everything: *"This is the Day in which God's most excellent favors have been poured out upon men, the Day in which His most mighty grace hath been infused into all created things."*[7]

This Day of God is a call for humanity to awake from its stupor. Recognizing and embracing the Prophet for this Day surpass any benefits on earth: *"Take ye advantage of the Day of God. Verily, to meet Him is better for you than all that whereon the sun shineth, could ye but know it."*[8]

And not only does humanity benefit by recognizing the Prophet of this Day, but it has a duty to do so: *"The whole duty of man in this Day is to attain that share of the flood of grace which God poureth forth for him."*[9]

The road to delightful springtime is difficult because winter—corruption and materialism, wars and atrocities, racism and sexism, environmental degradation, greed and the profit motive—tries to hang on. This retrenchment results in worsening troubles and sorrows. The accelerating momentum of the spiritual energies released by the Dispensation of Bahá'u'lláh have been provoking ingrained reactionary forces for more than 150 years. The temporary result is the disintegration of society and its moral standards. But take heart. Bahá'u'lláh wrote: *"Soon will the present-day order be rolled up, and a new one spread out in its stead. Verily, thy Lord speaketh the truth, and is the Knower of things unseen."*[10]

Humanity has journeyed spiritually through the Adamic Cycle that started with Adam and ended with Muhammad. Figuratively speaking, mankind has passed through various levels of spiritual childhood and has been experiencing the turbulence of adolescence, which include glimpses of maturity. These are now the early years of the Cycle of Fulfillment that started in 1844 with a new chapter in God's plan. As humanity tries to emerge from its rebellions and poor choices to attain maturity, the pace of its development accelerates as does the pace of opposing forces. The seeming quickening of time started imperceptibly and has steadily increased until today it seems breathless. Calendars and clocks have not changed. The earth circles the sun as it always has. But the forces of human life and events have accelerated almost beyond comprehension. Hence, chaos. The effects of the Day of God are increasingly felt in a deep and immediate sense.

The drawn-out death throes of a society disintegrating in disruptive, violent, and chaotic ways is analogous to the proverbial sinner clinging to life on his deathbed because he fears meeting his Maker. Individuals aligned with the forces of darkness may not be consciously aware of the new energies permeating the earth, but when they perceive the changes, they scramble like bugs when a rotting log is lifted.

It's also possible to consider today's turmoil like two lines on a graph. Visualize the energy of this Day of God as a line gradually rising from the bottom left corner up toward the top right, and the disintegration of society and its institutions as a line gradually moving from the top left corner of the graph down to the bottom right. Tension and chaos increase as the lines gain momentum and approach each other. At some point, these two lines will cross. That may be the time of *"great distress, unequaled from the beginning of the world until now— and never to be equaled again."* (Matthew 24:21)

Future historians may well label as "unequalled" in history the time of convergence of the two lines on the graph. The nadir of this experience may make the limbs of mankind quake. Nevertheless, an apex has been promised. Humanity will progress spiritually toward the goal of ushering in the Kingdom of God on earth.

Epilogue

We have examined the nineteenth-century convergences in prophecy for Judaism, Christianity, Islam, and the Baha'i Faith. Now, we will focus on the soul and dreams because Miller had a most interesting dream a couple of years before his death. Bahá'u'lláh shared some interesting truths about dreams:

> *Know thou of a truth that the worlds of God are countless in their number, and infinite in their range. Consider thy state when asleep. Verily, I say, this phenomenon is the most mysterious of the signs of God amongst men … the world in which thou livest is different and apart from that which thou hast experienced in thy dream. This latter world hath neither beginning nor end. … thy spirit, having transcended the limitations of sleep and having stripped itself of all earth attachment, hath, by the act of God, been made to traverse a realm which lieth hidden in the innermost reality of this world.*[1]

The Baha'i Faith teaches that our immortal souls come into being at conception of the physical body. However, the human soul is not contained within the body but instead is associated with it. Our souls often go to work while we sleep to obtain a better understanding of complex issues confronting us during waking hours and to find solutions for them. During sleep, our souls work to heal our disappointments and sorrows of life, to give spiritual balm to our emotional and mental wounds. Our dreams often reflect our souls' travels and learning.

'Abdu'l-Bahá said that the soul has two modes of operation while we are alive. The first is through the mediation of bodily instruments and organs. For example, the soul sees through the eyes, hears through the ears, and speaks with the tongue.[2] The second mode gives the soul far more freedom while the body is unconscious or asleep:

> *The other mode of the spirit's influence and action is without these bodily instruments. For example, in the state of sleep, it sees without the eyes, it hears without ears, it speaks without a tongue, it runs without feet—in brief, all these powers are exerted without the mediation of instruments and organs. How often it happens that the spirit has a dream in the realm of sleep whose purport comes to be exactly materialized two years hence! Likewise, how often it happens that in the world of dreams the spirit solves a problem that it could not solve in the realm of wakefulness. Awake, the eye sees only a short distance, but in the realm of dreams one who is in the East may see the West.*
>
> *While asleep, this physical body is as dead: It neither sees, nor hears, nor feels, and it has neither consciousness nor perception—its powers are suspended. Yet the spirit is not only alive and enduring but also exerts a greater influence, soars to loftier heights, and possesses a deeper understanding.[3]*

Miller remained stalwart in his Adventist faith, but as his health declined "he was very much pained by the irregularities, extravagances, and strange notions practiced or entertained by those who had departed from his teachings and counsels."[4] Miller wrote to his close friend Himes on December 3, 1847: "While in this deplorable state of mind, when I was about to believe in the total depravity of all men, and that all profession of religion was nothing but hypocrisy, I received comfort and consolation from the following, which may pass for 'A Dream.'"[5] Although the dream is long, it reads easily.

> I dreamed that God, by an unseen hand, sent me a curiously wrought casket, about ten inches long by six square, made of ebony and pearls curiously inlaid. To the casket there was a key attached. I immediately took the key and opened the casket, when, to my wonder and surprise, I found it filled with all sorts and sizes of jewels, diamonds, and precious stones, and gold and silver coin of every dimension and value, beautifully arranged in their several places in the casket, and thus arranged, they reflected a light and glory equaled only by the sun.

> I thought it was my duty not to enjoy this wonderful sight alone, although my heart was overjoyed at the brilliancy, beauty, and value of its contents. I therefore placed it on a centre-table in my room, and gave out word that all who had a desire might come and see the most glorious and brilliant sight ever seen by man in this life.

> The people began to come in, at first few in number, but increasing to a crowd. When they first looked

into the casket they would wonder and shout for joy. But when the spectators increased every one would begin to trouble the jewels, taking them out of the casket and scattering them on the table.

I began to think the owner would require the casket and jewels again at my hand; and if I suffered them to be scattered, I could never place them in their places in the casket again as before; and felt I should never be able to meet the accountability, for it would be immense. I then began to plead with the people not to handle them, not take them out of the casket; but the more I plead, the more they scattered; — and now they seemed to scatter them all over the room, on the floor, and on every piece of furniture in the room.

I then saw that among the genuine jewels and coin they had scattered an innumerable quantity of spurious jewels and counterfeit coin. I was highly incensed at their base conduct and ingratitude, and reproved and reproached them for it; but the more I reproved the more they scattered the spurious jewels and false coin among the genuine.

I then became vexed in my very soul, and began to use physical force to push them out of the room; but while I was pushing out one, three more would enter, and bring in dirt, and shavings, and sand, and all manner of rubbish, until they covered every one of the true jewels, diamonds, and coins, which were all excluded from sight. They also tore in pieces my casket, and scattered it among the rubbish. I thought no man regarded my sorrow or my anger. I became wholly discouraged and disheartened, and sat down and wept.

While I was thus weeping and mourning for my great loss and accountability, I remembered God, and earnestly prayed that he would send me help.

Immediately the door opened, and a man entered the room, when the people all left it; and he, having a dirt brush in his hand, opened the windows, and began to brush the dust and rubbish from the room.

I cried to him to forbear, for there were some precious jewels scattered among the rubbish.

He told me to "fear not"' for he would "take care of them."

Then, while he brushed, the dust and rubbish, false jewels and counterfeit coin, all rose and went out of the windows like a cloud, and the wind carried them away. In the bustle I closed my eyes for a moment; when I opened them, the rubbish was all gone. The precious jewels, the diamonds, the gold and silver coins, lay scattered in profusion all over the room.

He then placed on the table a casket, much larger and more beautiful than the former, and gathered up the jewels, the diamonds, the coins, by the handful, and cast them into the casket, till not one was left, although some of the diamonds were not bigger than the point of a pin.

He then called upon me to "come and see."

I looked into the casket, but my eyes were dazzled with the sight. They shone with ten times their former glory. I thought they had been scoured in the sand by the feet of those wicked persons who had scattered and trod them in the dust. They were arranged in beautiful order in the casket, every one in its place, without any visible pains of the man who cast them in. I shouted with very joy, and that shout awoke me.

The effect of this on my mind has been extremely consoling and happy. Write to me the interpretation, and receive my love for you and yours.[6]

Himes published Miller's dream in the *Advent Herald* and received many responses to the request for interpretations, most of which reflected Adventist beliefs.

Dreams (and visions) are usually meaningful only to the person who receives them. Then to complicate matters, dreams may have more than one level of meaning. Add to these considerations the fact that the dreamer may or may not receive and remember dreams accurately, and that the subconscious needs and vain imaginings of the dreamer may interfere with valid interpretations as dreams filter through the brain. Shoghi Effendi gave perspective on these considerations:

> *That truth is often imparted through dreams no one who is familiar with history, especially religious history, can doubt. At the same time, dreams and visions are always coloured and influenced more or less by the mind of the dreamer and we must beware of attaching too much importance to them. The purer and more free from prejudice and desire our hearts and minds become, the more likely it is that our dreams will convey reliable truth, but if we have strong prejudices, personal liking and aversions, bad feelings or evil motives, these will*

warp and distort any inspirational impression that comes to us.[7]

Miller's dream was probably sent to give him consolation and perhaps to impart to him a higher truth than his conscious mind could handle. I hope that Miller was met by his Lord Jesus when he passed over into the worlds of God and that he was told the dream's meaning. He is undoubtedly now taking full advantage of every opportunity to learn and explore. I look forward to meeting him when my time on earth has been fulfilled.

A Pen Portrait of Bahá'u'lláh

Professor Edward Granville Browne, the distinguished orientalist of the University of Cambridge, visited Bahá'u'lláh at Bahji in the year 1890. He recorded his impressions of this momentous visit (below), which were then published in 'Abdu'l-Bahá's book *A Traveller's Narrative Written to Illustrate the Episode of the Báb* (Introduction, xxxix–xl). Browne translated that book from Persian into English.

Of the culminating event of this my journey some few words at least must be said. During the morning of the day after my installation at Behjé one of Behá's younger sons entered the room where I was sitting and beckoned to me to follow him. I did so, and was conducted through passages and rooms at which I scarcely had time to glance to a spacious hall, paved, so far as I remember (for my mind was occupied with other thoughts) with a mosaic of marble. Before a curtain suspended from the wall of this great ante-chamber my conductor paused for a moment while I removed my shoes. Then, with a quick movement of the hand, he withdrew, and, as I passed, replaced the curtain; and I found myself in a large apartment, along the upper end of which ran a low divan, while on the side opposite to the door were placed two or three chairs. Though I dimly suspected whither I was going and whom I was to behold (for no distinct intimation had been given to me), a second or two lapsed ere, with a throb of wonder and awe, I became definitely conscious that the room was not untenanted. In the corner where the divan met the wall sat a wondrous and venerable figure, crowned with a felt head-dress of the kind called táj by dervishes (but of unusual height and make), round the base of which was wound a small white turban. The face of him on whom I gazed I can never forget, though I cannot describe it. Those piercing eyes seemed to read one's very soul; power and authority sat on that ample brow; while the deep lines on the forehead and face implied an age which the jet-black hair and beard flowing down in indistinguishable luxuriance almost to the waist seemed to belie. No need to ask in whose presence I stood, as I bowed myself before one who is the object of a devotion and love which kings might envy and emperors sigh for in vain!

A mild dignified voice bade me be seated, and then continued: *"Praise be to God that thou hast attained!... Thou hast come to see a prisoner and an exile.... We desire but the good of the world and the happiness of the nations; yet they deem us a stirrer up of strife and sedition worthy of bondage and banishment.... That all nations should become one in faith and all men as brothers; that the bonds of affection and unity between the sons of men should be strengthened; that diversity of religion should cease, and differences of race be annulled*

- what harm is there in this?... Yet so it shall be; these fruitless strifes, these ruinous wars shall pass away, and the 'Most Great Peace' shall come.... Do not you in Europe need this also? Is not this that which Christ foretold?... Yet do we see your kings and rulers lavishing their treasures more freely on means for the destruction of the human race than on that which would conduce to the happiness of mankind.... These strifes and this bloodshed and discord must cease, and all men be as one kindred and one family.... Let not a man glory in this, that he loves his country; let him rather glory in this, that he loves his kind...."

Such, so far as I can recall them, were the words which, besides many others, I heard from Behá. Let those who read them consider well with themselves whether such doctrines merit death and bonds, and whether the world is more likely to gain or lose by their diffusion.

"Important Truths"
adopted by the Albany Conference

The following document was drawn up by a committee of twelve, including William Miller and Joshua Himes, that was appointed by the 61 delegates to the Albany Conference of April 1845. The delegates unanimously adopted this statement on the third and last day of the Conference. The statement "Important Truths" is cited from Memoirs of William Smith *by Sylvester Bliss, 304 to 308. In Boston, the* Advent Herald *and* Signs of the Times Reporter, *Vol. 9, no. 14, May 15, 1845, published a full account of the Albany conference, including the document "Important Truths." A complete report on the Albany conference is online at https:// archive.org/details/*

Important Truths

1

That the heavens and earth which are now, by the word of God, kept in store, reserved unto fire against the day of judgment and perdition of ungodly men. That the day of the Lord will come as a thief in the night, in which the heavens shall pass away with a great noise, and the elements shall melt with fervent heat; the earth also, and the works that are therein, shall be burned up. That the Lord will create new heavens and a new earth wherein righteousness—that is, the righteous—will forever dwell (2 Peter 3:7, 10, 11). And that the kingdom and the dominion under the whole heaven shall be given to the people of the saints of the Most High, whose kingdom is an everlasting kingdom, and all dominions shall serve and obey him (Hebrews 9:28).

2

That there are but two advents or appearings of the Saviour to this earth (Hebrews 9:28). That both are personal and visible (Acts 1:9, 11). That the first took place in the days of Herod (Matthew 2:1) when He was conceived of the Holy Ghost (Matthew 1:18), born of the Virgin Mary (Matthew 1:25), went about doing good (Matthew 11:5), suffered on the cross, the just for the unjust (1 Peter 3:18), died (Luke 23:46), was buried (Luke 23:56), arose again on the third day, the first fruits of them that slept (1 Corinthians 15:4), and ascended into the heavens (Luke 24:51), which must receive him until the times of the restitution of all things, spoken of by the mouth of all the holy prophets (Acts 3:21). That the Second Coming or appearing will take place when he shall descend from heaven, at the sounding of the last trumpet, to give his people rest (1 Thessalonians 4:16, 17; 1 Corinthians 15:52), being revealed from heaven in flaming fire, taking vengeance on them that know not God, and obey not the Gospel (2 Thessalonians 1:7, 8). And that he will judge the quick and the dead at his appearing and kingdom (2 Timothy 4).

3

That the Second Coming or appearing is indicated to be now emphatically nigh, even at the doors (Matthew 24:33), by the chronology of the prophetic periods (Daniel 7:25; 8:14; 9:24; 12:7, 11, 12; Revelation 9:10, 15; 11:2, 3; 12:6, 14; 13:5), the fulfillment of prophecy (Daniel 2nd, 7th, 8th, 9th, 11th, and 12th chaps; Revelation 9th, 11th, 12th, 13th, 14th, and 17th chaps.), and the signs of the times (Matthew 24:29; Luke 21:25, 16). And that this truth should be preached both to saints and sinners, that the first may rejoice, knowing their redemption draweth nigh (Luke 21:28; 1 Thessalonians 4:18), and the last be warned to flee from the wrath to come (2 Corinthians 5:11) before the Master of the house shall rise up and shut the door (Luke 13:24, 25).

4

That the condition of salvation is repentance toward God, and faith in our Lord Jesus Christ (Acts 20:21; Mark 1:15). And that those who have repentance and faith will live soberly, and righteously, and godly, in this present world, looking for that blessed hope, and the glorious appearing of the great God and our Saviour Jesus Christ (Titus 2:11–13).

5

That there will be a resurrection of the bodies of all the dead (John 5:28, 29), both of the just and the unjust (Acts 24:15). That those who are Christ's will be raised at his coming (1 Corinthians 15:23). That the rest of the dead will not live again until after a thousand years (Revelation

20:5). And that the saints shall not all sleep, but shall be changed in the twinkling of an eye at the last trump (1 Corinthians 15:51, 52).

6

That the only millennium taught in the Word of God is the thousand years which are to intervene between the first resurrection and that of the rest of the dead, as inculcated in the 20th of Revelation (Revelation 20:2–7). And that the various portions of Scripture which refer to the millennial state are to have their fulfillment after the resurrection of all the saints who sleep in Jesus (Isaiah 11; 35:1, 2, 5–10; 65:17–25).

7

That the promise, that Abraham should be the heir of the world, was not to him, or to his seed, through the law, but through the righteousness of faith (Romans 4:13). That they are not all Israel which are of Israel (Romans 9:6). That there is no difference, under the Gospel dispensation, between Jew and Gentile (Romans 10:12). That the middle wall of partition that was between them is broken down, no more to be rebuilt (Ephesians 2:14, 15). That God will render to every man according to his deeds (Romans 2:6). That if we are Christ's, then we are Abraham's seed, and heirs, according to the promise (Galatians 3:29). And that the only restoration of Israel, yet future, is the restoration of the saints to the earth, created anew, when God shall open the graves of those descendants of Abraham who died in faith, without receiving the promise, with the believing Gentiles, who have been grafted in with them into the same olive tree; and shall cause them to come up out of their graves, and bring them, with the living, who are changed, into the land of Israel (Ezekiel 37:12; Hebrews 11:12, 13; Romans 11:17; John 5:28, 29)

8

That there is no promise of this world's conversion (Matthew 24:14). That the Horn of Papacy will war with the saints, and prevail against them, until the Ancient of Days shall come, and judgement be given to the saints of the Most High, and the time come that the saints possess that kingdom (Daniel 7: 21, 22). That the children of the kingdom, and the children of the wicked one, will continue together until the end of the world, when all things that offend shall be gathered out of the kingdom, and the righteous shall shine forth as the sun in the kingdom of their Father (Matthew 13:37–43). That the Man of Sin will only be destroyed by the brightness of Christ's coming (2 Thessalonians 2:8). And that the nations of those which are saved and redeemed to God by the blood of Christ, out of every kindred, and tongue, and people, and nation, will be made kings and priests unto God, to reign forever on the earth (Revelation 5:9, 10; 21:24).

9

That it is the duty of the ministers of the Word to continue in the work of preaching the Gospel to every creature, even unto the end (Matthew 28: 19, 20), calling upon them to repent, in view of the fact that the kingdom of heaven is at hand (Revelation 14:7); that their sins may be blotted out when the times of refreshing shall come from the presence of the Lord (Acts 3: 19, 20).

That the departed saints do not enter their inheritance, or receive their crowns, at death (Daniel 12:13; Revelation 6:9–11; Romans 8:22, 23). That they without us cannot be made perfect (Hebrews 11:40). That their inheritance, incorruptible and undefiled, and that fadeth not away, is reserved in heaven, ready to be revealed in the last time (1 Peter 1:4, 5). That there are laid up for them and us crowns of righteousness, which the Lord, the righteous Judge, shall give at the day of Christ to all that love his appearing (2 Timothy 4:3). That they will only be satisfied when they awake in Christ's likeness (Psalm 17:15). And that, when the Son of Man shall come in his glory, and all the holy angels with him, the King will say to those on his right hand, "Come, ye blessed of my Father, inherit the kingdom prepared for you from the foundations of the world" (Matthew 25:34). Then they will be equal to the angels, being the children of God and of the resurrection (Luke 20:36).

The Remarkable Parallel:
Jesus and the Báb

The following is quoted from Thief in the Night, or, The Strange Case of the Missing Millennium *by William Sears, 87–89.*

I began searching the libraries for all the available documents. You can imagine my feelings of awe and wonder when I uncovered the following facts. The death of this young man [the Báb] occurred in July 1850. He was slain publicly because of his words and his teaching. Everything I learned about his life reminded me of Christ. In fact, after carefully searching into his background, I could find but one parallel in all recorded history to his brief, turbulent career; only the moving story of the passion of Jesus Christ himself. As part of my record of 'findings', I here set down the remarkable similarity in the story of their lives:

1. They were both youthful.
2. They were both known for their meekness and loving kindness.
3. They both performed healing miracles.
4. The period of their ministry was very brief in each case, and moved with dramatic swiftness to its climax.

5. Both of them boldly challenged the time-honoured conventions, laws and rites of the religions into which they had been born.

6. They courageously condemned the unbridled graft and corruption that they saw on every side, both religious and secular.

7. The purity of their own lives shamed the people among whom they taught.

8. Their chief enemies were among the religious leaders of the land. These officials were the instigators of the outrages they were made to suffer.

9. They both had indignities heaped upon them.

10. They were both forcibly brought before the government authorities and were subject to public interrogation.

11. They were both scourged following this interrogation.

12. They both went, first in triumph then in suffering, through the streets of the city where they were to be slain.

13. They were both paraded publicly, and heaped with humiliation, on the way to their place of martyrdom.

14. They both spoke words of hope and promise to the one who was to die with them; in fact, almost the exact same words: 'Thou shalt be with me in paradise.'

15. They were both martyred publicly before the hostile gaze of the onlookers who crowded the scene.

16. A darkness covered the land following their slaying, in each case beginning at noon.

17. Their bodies were both lacerated by soldiers at the time of their slaying.

18. They both remained in ignominious suspension before the eyes of an unfriendly multitude.

19. Their bodies came finally into the hands of their loving followers.

20. When their bodies, in each case, had vanished from the spot where they had been placed, the religious leaders explained away the fact.

21. Only a handful of their followers were with them at the times of their deaths.

22. In each case, one of their chief disciples denied knowing them. This same disciple, in each case, later became a hero.

23. Each of them had an outstanding woman follower who played a dramatic part in making the disciples turn their faces from the past and look toward the future.

24. Confusion, bewilderment and despair seized their followers in each case, following their martyrdom.

25. Through their disciples (the Peters and Pauls of each age) their Faiths were carried to all parts of the world.

26. They both replied with the same exact words to the question: Are you the Promised One?

27. Each of them addressed their disciples, charging them to carry their messages to the ends of the earth.

"What Is an Advent Christian?" by David Burge

In keeping with the copyright requirements for quoting from the article "What Is an Advent Christian?" in Chapter 11, the entire article is given below.

99.9% of Advent Christian beliefs are those we hold in common with Christians of all denominations, across all ages. We believe that salvation comes only by accepting Christ as our Sin bearer, Saviour, and Sovereign. Yet some of the things that Advent Christians believe do set us apart. We don't say these things make us "more Christian" than any other Believers. But we do see these issues as important enough to us to take a stand on them.

The Issues

Years ago a number of Christian groups chose the term "Advent" as part of their name to express their belief in certain Scriptural truths. Many Christian creeds, confessions of faith, theories and traditions were in conflict with the Bible. It was (and still is) widely taught: that the prophesies of the Second Coming of Christ are fulfilled "spiritually" in the history of the church; there will be a "golden age" of peace lasting at least 1000 years before the resurrection and judgment; that the dead go immediately to heaven or hell and are now enjoying or suffering their reward; and that heaven is the final abode of all the saints. These ideas were found to be without Scriptural foundation. Out of a desire to proclaim the truths of Scripture the Advent Christian movement was born.

Looking for His Coming

The hope of Christians is that Jesus will come again. But if at least 1000 years of universal peace is to be enjoyed before the resurrection and judgment, in what sense can we watch, or wait with baited breath, looking for his Coming? It is true that a probable year for Christ's return was fixed upon by many early Adventists. This was wrong. Many repented. But it was not their choice of a year for the end that has been of enduring significance. What has endured is their witness to the truths of Christ's personal coming to judge the living and the dead, and to establish his reign upon a renewed earth, and that this coming is imminent, not necessarily separated from us by a thousand or more years.

Most Christians today look for a literal, physical coming of Jesus Christ to the earth. Many believe this coming may be soon. Advent Christians played a big part in rescuing this truth from obscurity.

Only God is Immortal

Many people believe human beings have an immortal soul. That John Brown's body lies a-mouldering in the grave, but his soul goes marching on. The Bible says God alone is immortal. The Bible says human beings are "dust and ashes".

To be immortal is to be death-proof. We are not death-proof. We die. Body and soul. Lock, stock and barrel.

There is nothing left to go marching on with. When God made Adam, he made a body of dust. He breathed into him the breath of life and Adam became a living soul. A living soul is not an immortal one. At death the body returns to dust and the spirit, or the breath of life, returns to God who gave it. Without the breath of life the whole person is dead.

Life Only In Christ

We call our belief "life only in Christ" or "Conditional Immortality". The Bible teaches that we do not go to heaven or hell at death. Immortality is something we must seek after and only the righteous will be given immortality by Jesus Christ at His Coming. Since it is only by faith in Jesus Christ that people are granted immortality we may say that God has made immortality conditional upon faith in Christ. That is why we call this belief "life only in Christ" or "Conditional Immortality".

Death: Friend or Foe?

For the Greeks salvation was to escape the body altogether. For them death was something less than an unqualified disaster. Something to look forward to. Yet when Jesus heard that his friend Lazarus was dead, he didn't mouth pious platitudes about his being "promoted to glory". Nor did he speak of Lazarus as having "gone to a better place". He wept!

Those who deny all possibility of a future life tell us that at death we simply sink into oblivion. Those who believe in the immortality of the soul often speak of death as a doorway to a better place. The Bible however speaks of death as "the last enemy" to be defeated only when Christ comes again.

This World is Good – The Next is Better

The idea that the soul is "spiritual" and the body isn't implies to many people that Creation itself is un-spiritual, even distasteful. The Greeks spoke of the body as the prison house of the soul. They thought of this material creation as second rate. The Bible, on the other hand, sees the body, and the material world in general, as good and glorious. How could it be otherwise? It was made by a good and glorious God. And the Bible affirms that, in spite of everything, God prizes his Creation enough to make a revised version of all things.

Hell is not a cosmic torture chamber. It is a Divine garbage dump. It is an incinerator in which all that is sinful or imperfect about this world – all who are in rebellion against God – will be finally destroyed when this world is made new. Then – whatever else "heaven" may include – believers will live forever with God and Christ in a whole new and improved universe in which only righteousness will dwell.

A Resurrection Hope

Many believe that it is only natural for every human being to go on living after death. But there is nothing about the way we are made that enables us to live on and on. All the earliest Christian creeds affirmed the belief that the future life comes only by means of the resurrection of the body.

Resurrection is a super-natural work of God. We go to our graves as dead as dead can be. We can only go on living beyond the grave if we are given our lives back again. This is just what God intends to do. He will give us back our lives, just as he gave life to us in the first place, at the resurrection. Our resurrection hope is not a blind leap of faith. Jesus has been there and done that! Because he lives we can know that we shall live also.

SO ... What?

These Advent Christian distinctives are God-honouring, and Christ-centred. Our God is not a cosmic torturer, worse even than Hitler or any human tyrant. There is nothing within us that will enable us to live beyond death. If there is any hope for the future it must be found in Christ alone!

Christ is much more than a spiritual referee, a mere sorter of souls, sending some "up" and some "down". He is the Resurrection and the Life. Upon him and his coming depend the resurrection, the reward of the righteous, the abolition of sin and its consequences, the renewal and perfection of the earth.

He is our only hope. He is all we need. He is all the world needs.

APPENDIX E

Basic Principles of the Baha'i Faith

'Abdu'l-Bahá presented the basic and distinguishing principles of the Faith of Bahá'u'lláh during the course of his journeys in Europe and North America from 1910 to 1913. Shoghi Effendi wrote a summary of them in *God Passes By*, 281–82. He made it clear that these principles, together with the laws and ordinances revealed by Bahá'u'lláh in the *Kitáb-i-Aqdas*—the Most Holy Book of the Baha'i Dispensation—constitute the bedrock of God's latest Revelation to mankind.

It was in the course of these epoch-making journeys and before large and representative audiences, at times exceeding a thousand people, that 'Abdu'l-Bahá expounded, with brilliant simplicity, with persuasiveness and force, and for the first time in His ministry, those basic and distinguishing principles of His Father's Faith, which together with the laws and ordinances revealed in the Kitáb-i-Aqdas constitute the bed-rock of God's latest Revelation to mankind. The independent search after truth, unfettered by superstition or tradition; the oneness of the entire human race, the pivotal principle and fundamental doctrine of the Faith; the basic unity of all religions; the condemnation of all forms of prejudice, whether religious, racial, class or national; the harmony which must exist between religion and science; the equality of men and women, the two wings on which the bird of human-kind is able to soar; the introduction of compulsory education; the adoption of a universal auxiliary language; the abolition of the extremes of wealth and poverty; the institution of a world tribunal for the adjudication of disputes between nations; the exaltation of work, performed in the spirit of service, to the rank of worship; the glorification of justice as the ruling principle in human society, and of religion as a bulwark for the protection of all peoples and nations; and the establishment of a permanent and universal peace as the supreme goal of all mankind—these stand out as the essential elements of that Divine polity which He proclaimed to leaders of public thought as well as to the masses at large in the course of these missionary journeys.

Readers can investigate further aspects of the Faith through several websites. The official website of the Baha'i world community is http://www.bahai.org, and the official website of the Universal House of Justice is http://www.universalhouseofjustice.bahai.org.

Most texts of Baha'i scriptures published in English, as well as many Baha'i books and compilations, are searchable through http://www.bahai.org/library and http://www.bahai-library.com.

Notes

Introduction

1. The term *mulla* was a title of respect for an Islamic cleric, theologian, or judge learned in the Qur'an and Islamic law.

2. *The Báb, Selections from the Writings of the Báb,* Section 3:34, para. 1, 136–37.

3. These tablets are published in *The Summons of the Lord of Hosts.*

4. Letter dated June 6, 2013, from the Universal House of Justice to an individual, https://bahai-library.com/ uhj_numbers_sacred_writings

5. *Baha'i World News Service,* May 1, 2002, http://news.bahai.org/story/163. *The Baha'i World News Service* is the official news source of the worldwide Baha'i community.

6. 'Abdu'l-Bahá, *Tablets of 'Abdu'l-Bahá,* vol. 2, 430. The Blessed Perfection is one of the titles of Bahá'u'lláh.

7. Letter dated June 6, 2013, from the Universal House of Justice to an individual, https://bahai-library.com/ uhj_numbers_sacred_writings

8. These include, but are not limited to, *Some Answered Questions* by Laura Clifford Barney, a compilation of answers to questions she posed to him between 1904 and 1906; *Paris Talks,* speeches given while he was in Paris; *The Promulgation of Universal Peace: Talks Delivered by 'Abdul-Bahá during His Visit to the United*

States and Canada in 1912; and *Tablets of 'Abdu'l-Bahá: Volumes 1–3*.

9. Shoghi Effendi wrote *God Passes By*. Collections of his letters can be found in *The Advent of Divine Justice*, *The Promised Day Is Come*, and *The World Order of Bahá'u'lláh*.

10. Letter dated June 6, 2013, from the Universal House of Justice to an individual, http://bahai-library.com/uhj_numbers_sacred_writings

11. Cablegram dated September 26, 1957, from Shoghi Effendi to the Baha'i world, *Messages to the Baha'i World*, 127.

12. Letter dated December 2, 1957, to all National Assemblies from the Custodians of the Baha'i World Faith, *The Ministry of the Custodians 1957–1963: An Account of the Stewardship of the Hands of the Cause*, 40.

13. Letter dated March 9, 1965, from the Universal House of Justice to a National Spiritual Assembly, *Messages from the Universal House of Justice*, no. 23.4, 51.

14. Cablegram dated September 26, 1957, *Messages to the Baha'i World*, 127.

15. Bahá'u'lláh, *The Hidden Words*, no. 2 from the Arabic.

Chapter 1: Moving to Fever Pitch

1. Peter Feinman, "Itinerant Circuit-riding Minister: Warrior of Light in a Wilderness of Chaos," *Methodist History*. Vol. 45:1, October 2006.

2. Letter dated October 28, 1814, from William Miller to his wife, Lucy Miller. Cited by Sylvester Bliss, *Memoirs of William Miller*, 62.

3. Sylvester Bliss, *Memoirs of William Miller*, 73.

4. Ibid., 74–75.

5. *Cruden's Concordance*, a biblical index, was single-handedly created by Alexander Crudens (1699–1770) for the King James Bible. It was first published in 1737 and has never been out of print.

6. *Memoirs*, 87.

7. Ibid., 86.

8. Ibid., 97.

9. Ibid., 98.

10. Ibid., 87.

11. David T. Arthur, "James V. Himes and the Cause of Adventism," *The Disappointed: Millerism and Millenarianism in the Nineteenth Century*, 39.

12. George R. Knight, *Millennial Fever*, 83. Knight is a leading Seventh-day Adventist historian, writer, and educator who has been a best-selling and influential spokesperson for the Church. As of 2018, he was professor emeritus of church history at Andrews University, a Seventh-day Adventist university in Berrien Springs, Michigan.

13. *Millennial Fever*, 83.

14. Joshua V. Himes, comp., *Millennial Harp, or Second Advent Hymns: Designed for Meetings on the Second Coming of Christ*, 7. Cited in *Millennial Fever*, 81.

Chapter 2: The Prophet Daniel: 2,300 Days

1. The prophet Daniel saw himself in the province of Elam, Persia, when he was told about the 2,300 days (Daniel 8:14). *"In my vision I saw myself in the citadel of Susa in the province of Elam; in the vision I was beside the Ulai Canal."* (Daniel 8:2)

Chapter 3: A Frenzy of Preparation

1. Letter dated April 10, 1833, to Elder Hendryx from William Miller. Cited by Bliss, *Memoirs*, 112.

2. Carolyn Sparey Fox, *The Half Of It Was Never Told*, 108.

3. Report of Elder L. D. Fleming of Portland, Maine, after the visit of Miller from March 11 to 23, 1840. Cited by Bliss, *Memoirs*, 154–55.

4. *Memoirs*, 156.

5. Ibid., 80.

6. David L. Rowe, "Millerites: A Shadow Portrait," *The Disappointed*, 11. An endnote states that the sample consisted of a random ten percent computation of the entire census of Ithaca based on a selection of every tenth household. Dr. Rowe retired in May 2017 as a professor of religious history at Middle Tennessee State University in Murfreesboro. He has served as consultant on a series of documentaries for the Baha'i Faith and for scholars pursuing topics in Millerite history.

7. Ibid., 9–10.

8. Ibid., 10.

9. William Miller, *Signs of the Times*, January 25, 1843, 147. Cited by Bliss, *Memoirs*, 180.

10. William Miller, "Address to Believers in the Near Advent," January 1, 1843. Cited by Bliss, *Memoirs*, 182.

11. Moses Stuart, *Hints on the Interpretation of Prophecy*, 173. Cited by Knight, *Millennial Fever*, 140.

12. *Lowell Courier*, Lowell, Massachusetts, February 23, 1843. Cited in *The Midnight Cry*, 140, and Knight, *Millennial Fever*, 62–63.

13. William Miller, letter to Himes dated May 2, 1844. Cited by Bliss, *Memoirs*, 260.

14. William Miller, *Advent Herald*, March 6, 1844. Cited by Bliss, *Memoirs*, 265. The *Advent Herald* was published by Himes and was the new name for *Signs of the Times*.

15. Karaite Judaism is a small Jewish sect that recognizes only the Torah as the authority for religious law and theology and uses its own calendar, which varies from the Rabbinic calendar by a few days.

16. James White, *Sketches of the Christian Life and Public Labours of William Miller*, ch. 14. Cited by Fox, *The Half Of It Was Never Told*, 108–09.

Chapter 4: The Great Disappointment

1. *Advent Herald*, August 21, 1844, 20. Cited in Bliss, *Millennial Fever*, 200.

2. *True Midnight Cry*, August 22, 1844, 4; *Advent Herald*, August 21, 1844, 20. Cited in Bliss, *Millennial Fever*, 188.

3. Ibid.

4. Ibid., 190.

5. *Baltimore Sun*, October 25, 1844, cited by Francis Nichol, *The Midnight Cry*, 260, and by Knight, *Millennial Fever*, 217.

6. *Cleveland Plain Dealer*, October 30, 1844, 2. Cited by Knight, *Millennial Fever*, 217.

7. Gary E. Wait, "The End of the World," Dartmouth College Bulletin, November, 1993.

   Footnote no. 28: "Washington Morse, 'Remembrance of Former Days,' *Advent Review and Sabbath Herald*, 7 May 1901, p. 291, as cited by Nichol, *The Midnight Cry*, 248."

8. *Advent Herald,* January 8, 1845, 176. Cited by David T. Arthur, "Joshua V. Himes and the Cause of Adventism," *The Disappointed,* 56.

9. Letter from William Miller to Joshua Himes, November 10, 1844. Cited by Bliss, *Memoirs,* 280.

10. Letter from William Miller to the *Advent Herald,* December 3, 1844. Cited by Bliss, *Memoirs,* 283.

11. *Millennial Fever,* 245.

12. William Miller, "Address to the Brethren submitted to the Albany Conference," April 1845. Cited by Bliss, *Memoirs,* 312–14.

13. William Miller, "Address to the Public," *Advent Herald,* September 9, 1846. Cited by Bliss, *Memoirs,* 348–49.

14. Miller. Cited by Bliss, *Memoirs,* 370.

Chapter 5: Expectancy in the East

1. Hadiths are the remembered sayings of Muhammad and His companions that were not included in the Qur'an. Early in the history of Islam, the sayings of hadith were collected from people who had associated with Muhammad and claimed to have heard Him make the statements. The body of hadith is influential in Islamic belief and theology.

2. H. M. Balyuzi, *Muhammad and the Course of Islam,* 149–50.

3. Ibid., 153.

4. Nabíl-i-A'zam, *The Dawn-Breakers: Nabíl's Narrative of the Early Days of the Baha'i Revelation,* Introduction, li–liii. Excerpted from Lord Curzon, *Persia and the Persian Question,* vol. 1, 452–53.

Chapter 6: The Search in the East

1. *The Dawn-Breakers*, Introduction, xxxvii.
2. Cablegram dated June 21, 1932, from Shoghi Effendi to the American Baha'i community, *Messages to America*, 1.
3. *The Dawn-Breakers*, Introduction, xxxviii. Excerpted from Lord Curzon, *Persia and the Persian Question*, vol. 1, 433.
4. Shaykh was an honorific title for outstanding scholars of Islam.
5. *The Dawn-Breakers*, 1–2.
6. Ibid., 2.
7. 'Abdu'l-Bahá, *The Promulgation of Universal Peace*, 10.
8. *The Dawn-Breakers*, 4.
9. Ibid., 4–5.
10. The title *Siyyid* was bestowed upon all male descendants of Muhammad.
11 *The Dawn-Breakers*, 16.
12. *The Dawn-Breakers*, 24–25. In Shia Islamic tradition, Jábulqá and Jábulsá are the names for the mythic cities where the hidden Imam is believed to have been hiding and waiting. Siyyid Kazim was hinting that the advent would not be a literal return of the twelfth Imam, the Qa'im, but the coming of a new Prophet of God.
13. *The Dawn-Breakers*, Introduction, xlv-xlvi. Excerpted from Curzon, *Persia and the Persian Question*.
14. *The Dawn-Breakers*, 26–27. Green turbans were worn only by men descended from the Prophet Muhammad.
15. Ibid., 27.
16. Ibid., 28–29.

Chapter 7: 1844 Fulfilled

1. *The Dawn-Breakers*, 47–48.
2. Ibid., 52.
3. Ibid., 56.
4. Ibid., 57.
5. Ibid.
6. Ibid.
7. A *Surih* (or *Surah*) is a chapter in the Qur'an. There are 114 chapters in the Qur'an.
8. *The Dawn-breakers*, 59.
9. Ibid., 61.
10. Ibid. The Surih of Joseph is the largest exposition in the Qur'an on a person from the Hebrew Bible and, as such, it has great importance in Islam. The saga of Joseph also has great significance in the Baha'i Faith.
11. Ibid., 63.
12. The complete account can be read online in *The Dawn-breakers*, 52–66, www.bahai-library.com/nabil_dawnbreakers
13. Shoghi Effendi, *God Passes By*, 57-58.
14. Ibid., 58.
15. *Ulamas* were learned Islamic scholars. The Bábí and Baha'i Faiths found many of their most devoted believers and martyrs among the ulamas, as well as their most implacable enemies.
16. *The Dawn-Breakers*, 315–16 (emphasis added).
17. The Shrine of Bahá'u'lláh, the resting place for Bahá'u'lláh's earthly remains, is the most holy place for Baha'is. It is located in Bahji, a few miles outside the town of Akka, where He lived His last few years.
18. 'Abdu'l-Bahá, *Some Answered Questions*, no. 33.6, 150.

19. *God Passes By*, 276–77.

20. Bahá'u'lláh, *The Kitáb-i-Íqán*, para. 20, 21–22.

21. Ibid., para. 162, 153–54.

22. Ibid., para. 191, 176.

Chapter 8: Daniel: 70 Weeks and 1,260, 1,290, and 1,335 Days

1. *Some Answered Questions*, no. 10.13–14, 47–48.

2. Bahá'u'lláh, *Gleanings from the Writings of Bahá'u'lláh*, no. 61, 118–19. The Nightingale is a pseudonym for Bahá'u'lláh.

3. *Some Answered Questions*, no. 10.20, 50.

4. Ibid., no. 10.22, 50–51.

5. 'Abdu'l-Bahá, cited by Shoghi Effendi and Lady Blomfeld, "Tablet to a Kurdish Friend," *The Passing of 'Abdu'l-Bahá*, 24; *Lights of Guidance*, no. 1414, 432–33.

6. Letter written on behalf of the Guardian dated May 6, 1954, to the National Spiritual Assembly of Canada. *Messages to Canada*, 44.

Chapter 9: Muhammad, the Seal of the Prophets

1. *Gleanings*, no. 30, 74.

2. Ibid., no. 21, 50.

3. Ibid., no. 31, 74. In the Baha'i writings, the term Manifestation of God means Prophet of God.

4. *Some Answered Questions*, no. 41.4–5, 183.

5. Bahá'u'lláh, *Tablets of Bahá'u'lláh Revealed after the Kitáb-i-Aqdas*, 161–62.

6. *Gleanings*, no. 34, 81.

7. *Tablets of Bahá'u'lláh Revealed after the Kitáb-i-Aqdas*, 125.

Chapter 10: The Divine Springtime

1. United States Patent Activity Calendar Years 1790 to the present, https://www.uspto.gov/web/offices/ac/ido/oeip/taf/h_counts.htm

2. Patent Librarian's Notebook. https://patentlibrarian.com/2017/12/28/u-s-patent-statistics-and-numbers-for-2017

3. *Gleanings*, no. 99, 200.

Chapter 11: The Sectarian Survivors of Millerism

1. The Center for the Study of Global Christianity (CSGC), http://gordonconwell.edu/ockenga/research/documents/StatusofGlobalChristianity2017.pdf. The CSGC began a partnership with the Pew Research Center in 2008 with the launch of the World Religion Database. They work together to arrive at best estimates for the religious composition of countries. Pew relies on the CSGC to provide data on smaller countries and religious traditions where no survey data are available. The CSGC also collects data from religious communities themselves and relies on their self-identification as Christian.

2. David Burge, "What Is an Advent Christian?", Advent Christian Conference of New Zealand Inc., 2008. https://www.acconz.org.nz/links/publications-2/what-is-an-advent-christian

3. Ibid.

4. The data for 1990 was cited by Knight, *Millennial Fever*, 329, obtained from Kenneth Bedell and Alice M. Jones, eds., *Yearbook of American and Canadian Churches* (Nashville: Abingdon, 1992), 270–77.

5. The Association of Religion Data Archives, taken from the National Council of Churches Historic Archive CD. http://www.thearda.com/Denoms/D_1101.asp

6. Ibid. http://www.thearda.com/Denoms/D_1232.asp

7. Hiram Edson, undated manuscript of his life and experience, from J. N. Loughborough, "Apostolic and Adventist Compared," unpublished manuscript, 19–20. Cited by Knight, *Millennial Fever,* 305.

8. *Millennial Fever,* 302–03. The full vision as described by White is posted in full on the Seventh-day Adventist website "Digging for Truth." http://www.digging fortruth.org/article/76/prophecy/spirit-of-prophecy-section/visions-of-ellen-g-white/first-vision-dec-1844

9. Article 18, "28 Fundamental Beliefs," website of the Seventh-day Adventist Church. https://szu.adventist.org/wp-content/uploads/2016/04/28_Beliefs.pdf

10. 2017 Annual Statistical Report, 153rd Report of the General Conference of Seventh-day Adventists, 4. http://documents.adventistarchives.org/Statistics/ASR/ASR2017.pdf

Chapter 12: Understanding Matthew 24

1. Letter dated January 31, 1955, written on behalf of Shoghi Effendi to an individual believer, *The Bible: Extracts on the Old and New Testaments.*

2. *The Promulgation of Universal Peace,* 155.

3. *The Kitáb-i-Íqán* was written by Bahá'u'lláh in 1861 in response to questions from the maternal uncle of the Báb, who was a Muslim and had not yet recognized the station of his nephew.

4. Adib Taherzadeh, *The Revelation of Bahá'u'lláh*, vol. 1, 161–62. Adib Taherzadeh (1921–2000), a preeminent Baha'i scholar, was born and educated in Iran and pursued advanced engineering studies in England. He served on the National Spiritual Assemblies of the British Isles (1960–1971) and of Ireland (1972–76) and was then appointed to the European Board of Continental Counsellors, a senior advisory body in the Baha'i Faith. He later served on the Universal House of Justice (1988–2000).

5. *The Kitáb-i-Íqán*, para. 170, 159.

6. *The Promulgation of Universal Peace*, 208.

7. 'Adu'l-Bahá, *Paris Talks*, 80–81.

8. *The Kitáb-i-Iqán*, paras. 33–35, 36–37.

9. Ibid., para. 74, 66–67.

10. Ibid., para. 79, 71–72.

11. 'Abdu'l-Bahá, *Tablets of 'Abdu'l-Bahá*, vol. 3, 509.

12. Hushidar Motlagh, *I Shall Come Again*, 463. As of 2018, Dr. Motlagh is professor emeritus at Central Michigan University and has written about thirty books relating to the knowledge of God, understanding the Bible and the Qur'an, and the fulfillment of prophecies in the advent of the Baha'i Faith. His website can be found at https://globalperspective.org.

13. Ibid., 133.

Chapter 13: Bahá'u'lláh, the Glory of God

1. *The Promulgation of Universal Peace*, 145.

2. *Gleanings*, no. 51, 104.

3. *Tablets of Bahá'u'lláh Revealed After the Kitáb-i-Aqdas*, 164.

4. Bahá'u'lláh, cited by Shoghi Effendi, *The Promised Day is Come*, para. 279, 114.

5. *Gleanings*, no. 43, 94.

6. *Gleanings*, no. 10, 13. The Pen of the Most High is a title used sometimes for Bahá'u'lláh, but in this context it may refer to all the Prophets of God.

7. Ibid., no. 4, 6.

8. *The Kitáb-i-Aqdas*, no. 88, 52.

9. *Gleanings*, no. 5, 8.

10. Ibid., no. 4, 7.

Epilogue

1. *Tablets of Bahá'u'lláh Revealed After the Kitáb-i-Aqdas*, 187–88.

2. *Some Answered Questions*, no. 61.1, 261.

3. Ibid., no. 61.2–3, 261–62.

4. *Memoirs*, 358.

5. Ibid., 359.

6. Ibid., 359–61.

7. From a letter dated May 16, 1925 written on behalf of Shoghi Effendi to an individual. Cited in *Lights of Guidance*, no. 1739, 514–15.

Bibliography

Works of the Báb

Selections from the Writings of the Báb. Compiled by the Research Department of the Universal House of Justice. Trans. by Habib Taherzadeh with the assistance of a Committee at the Baha'i World Centre. Wilmette, IL: Baha'i Publishing Trust, 2006. Also available online, http://www.bahai.org/library/authoritative-texts/the-bab/selections-writings-bab

Works of Bahá'u'lláh

Epistle to the Son of the Wolf. Trans. by Shoghi Effendi. 1st pocket-size ed. Wilmette, IL: Baha'i Publishing Trust, 1988. Also available online, http://www.bahai.org/library/authoritative-texts/bahaullah/epistle-son-wolf

The Hidden Words. Trans. by Shoghi Effendi. Wilmette, IL: Baha'i Publishing Trust, 1985. Also available online, http://www.bahai.org/library/authoritative-texts/bahaullah/hidden-words

The Kitáb-i-Aqdas: The Most Holy Book. Haifa, Israel: Baha'i World Centre, 1993. Also available online, http://www.bahai.org/library/authoritative-texts/bahaullah/kitab-i-aqdas

Kitáb-i-Íqán (The Book of Certitude). Trans. by Shoghi Effendi. 1st pocket-size ed. Wilmette, IL: Baha'i Publishing Trust, 1983. Also available online, http://www.bahai.org/library/authoritative-texts/bahaullah/kitab-i-iqan

The Summons of the Lord of Hosts. Haifa, Israel: Baha'i World Centre, 2002. Also available online, http://www.bahai.org/library/authoritative-texts/ bahaullah/summons-lord-hosts

Tablets of Bahá'u'lláh Revealed after the Kitáb-i-Aqdas. Compiled by the Research Department of the Universal House of Justice. Trans. by Habib Taherzadeh et al. 1st pocket-size ed. Wilmette, IL: Baha'i Publishing Trust, 1988. Also available online, http://www.bahai.org/library/authoritative-texts/ bahaullah/tablets-bahaullah

Works of 'Abdu'l-Bahá

A Traveller's Narrative Written to Illustrate the Episode of the Báb. Trans. by E. G. Browne. London: Cambridge University Press, 1891 (two volumes). Reprinted 1974 (one volume). Wilmette, IL: Baha'i Publishing Trust, 1982. Also available online, http://www.bahai.org/library/authoritative-texts/ abdul-baha/travelers-narrative

The Promulgation of Universal Peace. Wilmette, IL: Baha'i Publishing Trust, 2nd edition, 1982. Also available online, http://www.bahai.org/library/ authoritative-texts/abdul-baha/promulgation- universal-peace

Some Answered Questions. Compiled and translated from the Persian by Laura Clifford Barney. Newly revised by a committee at the Baha'i World Centre. Haifa, Israel: Baha'i World Centre, 2014. Also available online, http://www.bahai.org/library/ authoritative-texts/abdul-baha/some-answered- questions

Tablets of 'Abdu'l-Bahá. 2nd ed. Chicago: Baha'i Publishing Society, 1919. Also available online, http://bahai-library.com/abdulbaha_tablets_abdulbaha

Tablets of the Divine Plan. Pocket size ed. Wilmette, IL: Baha'i Publishing Trust, 1993. Also available online, http://www.bahai.org/library/authoritative-texts/abdul-baha/tablets-divine-plan

Works of Shoghi Effendi

The Advent of Divine Justice. Wilmette, IL: Baha'i Publishing Trust, 1971. Also available online, http://www.bahai.org/library/authoritative-texts/shoghi-effendi/advent-divine-justice

God Passes By. Rev. ed. Wilmette, IL: Baha'i Publishing Trust, 1974. Also available online, http://www.bahai.org/library/authoritative-texts/shoghi-effendi/god-passes-by

Messages to America: Selected Letters and Cablegrams Addressed to the Bahá'is of North America, 1932–1946. Wilmette, IL: Baha'i Publishing Committee, 1947. Also available online, http://bahai-library.com/shoghieffendi_messages_america

Messages to Canada. Ottawa: Canada Baha'i Publishing Trust, 1965. Also available online, http://bahai-library.com/shoghieffendi_messages_canada

Messages to the Baha'i World. Wilmette, IL: Baha'i Publishing Trust, 1971. Also available online, http://bahai-library.com/writings/shoghieffendi/mbw/mbwall

The Passing of 'Abdu'l-Bahá. Shoghi Effendi and Lady Sara Blomfeld. Haifa, Israel: Rosenfeld Bros., 1922.

The Promised Day Is Come. 1st pocket-size ed. Wilmette, IL: Baha'i Publishing Trust, 1996. Also available online, http://www.bahai.org/library/authoritative-texts/shoghi-effendi/promised-day-come

The World Order of Bahá'u'lláh. 2nd rev. ed. Wilmette, IL: Baha'i Publishing Trust, 1974. Also available online, http://www.bahai.org/library/authoritative-texts/shoghi-effendi/world-order-bahaullah

Works of the Universal House of Justice

The Bible: Extracts on the Old and New Testament by Bahá'u'lláh, 'Adu'l-Bahá, Shoghi Effendi, and the Universal House of Justice. Compiled by the Research Department of the Universal House of Justice. http://bahai-library.com/uhj_old_new_testaments. Date unknown.

Messages from the Universal House of Justice 1963–1986: Third Epoch of the Formative Age. Compiled on behalf of Geoffrey Marks. Wilmette, IL: Baha'i Publishing Trust, 1996. Also available online, https://bahai-library.com/uhj_messages_1963_1986

The Ministry of the Custodians 1957–1963: An Account of the Stewardship of the Hands of the Cause. Haifa, Israel: Baha'i World Centre, 1992. Also available online, https://bahai-library.com/uhj_messages_1963_1986

Other

Arthur, David T., "James V. Himes and the Cause of Adventism." *The Disappointed: Millerism and Millenarianism in the Nineteenth Century.* Ronald L. Numbers and Jonathan M. Butler, eds. Knoxville, TN: University of Tennessee Press, 1993.

Balyuzi, H. M. *Bahá'u'lláh: The King of Glory*. London: George Ronald Publisher, 1980.

———. *Muhammad and the Course of Islam*. London: George Ronald Publisher, 1976.

Bliss, Sylvester. *Memoirs of William Miller*. Jasper, OR: Light Bearers Ministry, Advent Pioneer Books, 2015. Originally published by J. V. Himes, Boston, 1853.

Blomfeld, Lady Sara. *The Chosen Highway*. London: Baha'i Publishing Trust, 1940. Reprinted by George Ronald Publisher, 2007. Also available online, http://bahai-library.com/blomfield_chosen_highway

Burge, David. "What Is an Advent Christian?" Advent Christian Conference of New Zealand Inc, 2008. http://www.acconz.org.nz/links/publications-2/what-is-an-advent-christian

Cahill, Thomas. *The Gifts of the Jews: How a Tribe of Desert Nomads Changed the Way Everyone Thinks and Feels*. New York: Talese/Anchor Books, Hinges of History series, 1999.

Curzon, George N., Lord. *Persia and the Persian Question*, vol. 1. Also available online, https://bahai-library.com/curzon_persia_persian_question

Esslemont, J. E. *Bahá'u'lláh and the New Era: An Introduction to the Baha'i Faith*. 4th ed. Wilmette, IL: Baha'i Publishing Trust, 1980. Also available online, http://www.bahai.org/library/other-literature/publications-individual-authors/bahaullah-new-era/bahaullah-new-era.pdf?88a4646f

Feinman, Peter. "Itinerant Circuit-riding Minister: Warrior of Light in a Wilderness of Chaos." *Methodist History* 45:1, October 2006. http://archives.gcah.org/handle/10516/3218

Fox, Carolyn Sparey. *The Half Of It Was Never Told.* Oxford: George Ronald Publisher, 2015.

Himes, Joshua V., comp., *Millennial Harp, or Second Advent Hymns: Designed for Meetings on the Second Coming of Christ.* Boston: J. V. Himes, 1842.

Hornby, Helen Bassett, compiler. *Lights of Guidance: A Baha'i Reference File,* 3rd rev. ed. New Delhi, India: Baha'i Publishing Trust, 1994.

Knight, George R. *Millennial Fever and the End of the World: A Study of Millerite Adventism.* Nampa, ID: Pacific Press Publishing Association, 1993.

Miller, William. *Evidence from Scripture and History of the Second Coming of Christ About the Year 1843; and of His Personal Reign of One Thousand Years.* Brandon, VT: Vermont Telegraph Office, 1833. Also available online, https://archive.org/details/MillerW.EvidencesFromScriptureAndHistoryOfTheSecondComingOfChrist

_____. *Evidence from Scripture and History of the Second Coming of Christ About the Year 1843; Exhibited as a Course of Lectures.* Troy, NY: E. Gates, 1838; Boston: Joshua V. Himes, 1842; London: Forgotten Books, 2007. Also available online, http://www.earlysda.com/miller/evidence1.html

Morse, Washington. "Remembrance of Former Days," *Advent Review and Sabbath Herald,* Vol. 78, no. 19. May 7, 1901, 291. https://adventistdigitallibrary.org/adl-272276/adventist-review

Moses Stuart, *Hints on the Interpretation of Prophecy,* 2nd edition. New York: Van Nostrand & Terrett, 1851. Available online, https://www.preteristarchive.com/Books/pdf/1851_stuart_hints_interpretation.pdf

Motlagh, Hushidar. *I Shall Come Again, Vol. 1, Time Prophecies of the Second Coming,* 2nd ed. Mt. Pleasant, MI: Global Perspective, 2000.

Nabíl-i-A'zam. *The Dawn-breakers: Nabíl's Narrative of the Early Days of the Baha'i Revelation.* Trans. and ed. by Shoghi Effendi. Wilmette, IL: Baha'i Publishing Trust, 1932. Also available online, http://bahai-library.com/nabil_dawnbreakers

Numbers, Ronald L. and Jonathan M. Butler, Eds. *The Disappointed: Millerism and Millenarianism in the Nineteenth Century.* Knoxville, TN: The University of Knoxville Press, 1993.

Sears, William. *Thief in the Night, or, The Strange Case of the Missing Millennium.* Oxford: George Ronald Publisher, 1961. Also available online, http://bahai-library.com/sears_thief_night

Taherzadeh, Adib. *The Revelation of Bahá'u'lláh,* vol. 1. Oxford: George Ronald Publishers, 1977. All four volumes of this series are available online, http://www.studythefaith.com/at_rev.html

Wait, Gary E. "The End of the World." *Dartmouth College Library Bulletin.* November, 1993. http://www.dartmouth.edu/~library/Library_Bulletin/Nov1993/gewait

White, James. *Sketches of the Christian Life and Public Labours of William Miller.* Battle Creek, MI: Steam Press, 1875. Create Space Independent Publishing Platform, 2014. Also available online, http://www.centrowhite.org.br/files/ebooks/apl/all/JamesWhite/Sketches

Baha'i Websites

The Baha'i Encyclopedia Project,
    http://www.bahai-encyclopedia-project.org

The Baha'i Faith, an encyclopedia,
    https://www.bahaikipedia.org

The Baha'i Faith, website of the global Baha'i Community,
    http://www.bahai.org

Baha'i Reference Library, authoritative writings and
    guidance, http://www.bahai.org/library

Baha'i Films

Light to the World. The Universal House of Justice. Haifa,
    Israel: 2017. http://www.bahai.org/light-to-the-world

The Gate: Dawn of the Baha'i Faith. Produced by Spring
    Green Films and directed by Peabody Award-
    winning director Bob Hercules.
    https://www.thegatefilm.com

A Baha'i Vision. Radiant Century Productions.
    Los Altos, CA, 2017.
    https://www.youtube.com/watch?v=URUN9R3A_Bg

The Miller Prediction. Radiant Century Productions.
    Los Altos, CA, 2017.

    https://www.youtube.com/watch?v=GpRS8vvYGkg

The **Gate**

DAWN OF THE BAHA'I FAITH

SPRING GREEN FILMS PRESENTS "THE GATE" DIRECTED BY KEITH WALKER PRODUCED BY MARK BAHDY MUSIC BY YAAEL KING MONDSCHEIN EDITED BY PATRICIA FORDE DIRECTOR OF PHOTOGRAPHY ADAM MONDSCHEIN COSTUMES JAN SUTCLIFFE
EXECUTIVE PRODUCERS STEVE SAROWITZ, EDWARD A. PRICE, BOB HERCULES STORY BY STEVE SAROWITZ SCREENPLAY BY BOB HERCULES, EDWARD A. PRICE DIRECTED BY BOB HERCULES

192

Index

Printed in Great Britain
by Amazon